The Single Adult

Rev. Patrick Ireland O'Neill, O.S.A.

Paulist Press,
New York, N.Y.
Ramsey, N.J.

Photo Credits
  Cover Photo: Lou Niznik

  Craig Callan: 70
  Vivienne della Grotta: 46
  Robert Maust: 82
  Tom McCarthy: 2
  Rick Smolan: 16; 28; 58

Project Editor: Jean Marie Hiesberger
Designer: Emil Antonucci

Nihil Obstat
Msgr. Carroll E. Satterfield
Censor Librorum
Imprimatur
Most Rev. William D. Borders, D.D.
Archbishop of Baltimore
March 11, 1980

Library of Congress
Catalog Card Number: 79-92004

ISBN: 0-8091-2258-8

Published by Paulist Press
Editorial Office: 1865 Broadway, New York, N.Y. 10023
Business Office: 545 Island Road, Ramsey, N.J. 07446

Printed and bound in the
United States of America

To my Mom and Dad, who have helped me to understand the special value of being Christian and single, and to all those ministering with singles.

Contents

Follow Up Exercises by Kathleen G. Connolly

Singles:
A
Look
at
the
Past

As we grow into adulthood, we become more aware of those adults who were important to us in our childhood and who have influenced the way we grew up and, perhaps, the adult who we are today. The more obvious influences come to mind immediately: parents, grandparents, aunts and uncles, neighbors and family friends. For many of us, I suspect, there is one person who stands out as being unique among the rest. It might have been a brother, sister or cousin of one of our parents, or a family friend who was called "aunt" or "uncle" as a sign of affection. Aunt Alice (or Uncle Phil) was fun to be with, attentive to us, interesting, and usually arrived with little gifts for the children. What set Aunt Alice or Uncle Phil apart from the rest of the adults we knew was that he or she was not married, not a priest, not a member of a religious community. He or she was single in a world that as children we perceived as composed of married people and an occasional priest or religious.

Perhaps one day it struck us that Aunt Alice or Uncle Phil was single in a society where most people were part of a twosome. At that point we might have asked a parent why this was so. The usual answer was some variation on a common theme: (s)he hadn't met the right person yet, or stayed single out of a family need to care for an aging parent. Being single was thus defined as a state embraced because an opportunity for the other alternative, i.e., being married, had not presented itself. At some point later, we may have figured out (or been told) that the reason for Aunt Alice's or Uncle Phil's singleness was a little more complicated. It is not uncommon to hear of a person who entered into a disasterous early marriage, got a divorce, and then opted to remain single rather than enter into a second marriage not recognized by the Church. (Another variation on this is the person who fell in love with a divorced person and who maintained a "dating" relationship with that person for twenty or thirty years, again because of a reluctance to enter into a nonsacramental marriage.) Statistics tell us that some percentage of Aunt Alices and Uncle Phils never marry because they are homosexual. But these reasons aside, there remained adults who did not marry not because "the right one" did not come along, not because of an impediment to sacramental marriage, and not because of a homosexual orientation. These people remained single because they liked being single, they were happy being single, and if they thought about it in these categories, because they felt that God had called them to be single. And having answered that call, what did they find in terms of support from society and the Church?

It is not insignificant that one of the card games we first learned to play in childhood was called "Old Maid." All the cards in the deck were in pairs except for one—the Old Maid. The object of the game was to pick from each other's hands and get as many pairs as possible. But the ultimate objective, which in fact determined who won or lost, was not to get "stuck" with the Old Maid. That game mirrors several aspects of reality. The Old Maid is undesirable. Everyone else is in pairs, and that is acceptable. In society at large, it was easier and more acceptable to be an unmarried man than an unmarried woman. Unmarried women were referred to as "old maids" or "spinsters," neither of which has a particularly pleasant or attractive connotation. An unmarried man, of whatever age, is referred to as a "bachelor," a term that is at worst neutral and at best refers to a dashing man-about-town, a desirable addition to a dinner or party. The bachelor has "eluded capture." The old maid has been unable to "land" someone. It is interesting to note that an unmarried man who has developed eccentric habits as a result of living alone is sometimes referred to as an "old woman." If it was difficult to be single in a married society, the difficulty was twice as severe for women.

Society in the past tended to gear itself toward a world that is evenly divisible by two. If the single person could find few positive role models in the culture, perhaps the Church, which at least theoretically has recognized being single as a calling in life on a par with marriage and religious life, might offer some support and some guidance to the person who chooses to remain single.

Again, let's go back to our formative years to discover what our first impressions about states of life were all about. Most people probably remember May as vocation month perhaps with a particular Sunday designated as "Vocation Sunday." On this day, it was not unusual for a particular observance to be held that centered on vocations, and the emphasis was always on vocations to the religious life or the priesthood. In many places, this observance included a procession in which small children dressed up as priests or nuns. The implication could easily be drawn that the Church's major concern in the matter of vocations was the vocation to priesthood and religious life. Marriage was also mentioned (that was the vocation which, it was felt, most people would embrace), and the single life, once again, got little mention. Certainly we did not pray for vocations to the single state with the same fervor with which we prayed for religious vocations and the call to be good husbands and wives.

Within the Catholic high school system, there was an awareness that the graduating seniors would soon be facing choices regarding careers and their state in life. Students who looked like they might have a vocation, i.e., be called to the priesthood or the vowed life, often received personal attention from a priest, brother or sister. Again recognizing that the majority of students would probably opt for marriage, senior year religion courses made provision for discussions of marriage, often bringing in a married couple to talk about courtship, marriage, childrearing and sex. It was not considered a priority for students to be exposed to a single person who could talk from experience about being single. Once again, the Church put its highest priority on religious vocations, and pragmatically offered some form of education about marriage in view of the fact that most students would eventually marry. (Marriage education, too, sometimes left something to be desired. Often the married couple would not discuss family planning, citing either a reluctance to talk about their personal life, thereby denying the possibility of talking about sex objectively, or referring the question to the priest or sister conducting the session, since birth control was a moral question.)

This scenario is, of course, much more typical of the Church fifteen or twenty or twenty-five years ago than it is of the Church of our own day. Yet today we would still be more likely to find a marriage course than a singles course. Even our language, which expresses a basic understanding of how we see the world, reflects an orientation toward marriage even when we are speaking about those who are not married. We speak of single persons as being "unmarried," thereby defining them in terms of a state they have not chosen, in short, defining them negatively. The word "singles" itself is often used in a perjorative sense; witness the phrases "swinging singles," which denotes an irresponsible lifestyle and a prediliction toward "cheap" sex, and "single's bars," the places where swinging singles go to find partners for whatever kind of irresponsibility they are going to indulge in. We speak (usually negatively) of "premarital sex," which carries with it the assumption that the sexual act referred to takes place at some point prior to marriage, even though in many cases the partners, if they marry at all, do not end up marrying each other.

There is a parallel here with the criticism that is railed against feminists who seek to replace words such as "chairman" with the word "chairperson." The critics argue that it's *only* a word, that we all know that when someone refers to "mankind" that he or she *really* means men and women. What such critics fail to realize is that language usually does more than point out a specific object or person; by the way we do this pointing out we say something about our attitude toward what is being referred to. Language, verbal and non-verbal, precedes behavior. The speaker who says "mankind" may well be referring to the entire human race, but in making the reference in that way, the speaker is referring to the human race primarily in terms of one segment of the population. Certain racial and ethnic labels have a perjorative meaning attached to them, and we would be hard pressed to excuse a word such as "nigger" with the explanation that "everyone knows we're just referring to Black Americans." While generic terms such as "man" and "mankind" may not have that same kind of negative connotation, they do convey a sense that *all* of humanity can be spoken of in terms of what is approximately 49% of the population. And in that sense, they are negative phrases because they define some people (women) in terms of what they are not (men).

In the same way our definition of single people in terms of what they are not (married) betrays our attitude about the value of being single. We are saying that being single does not have much positive value, that we can only speak about it in terms of what it is not. To call single people "single" and not "unmarried" is to admit that being married is not the goal of everyone's existence and that being single has a value independent of another state in life. To speak of sexual intercourse between single people, and not to use the terms "premarital sex" and "sex outside of marriage" is to admit that sexual activity does take place between people who are single and who may never get married, much less to each other. Perhaps as Church we do not want to admit this at all, much less have to deal with it.

Likewise, cleansing the term "singles" of its baser meanings will be a recognition of the fact that our stereotypes of single people are as meaningless and as evil as are the racial and ethnic stereotypes of a white, Anglo-Saxon society. Only by ridding ourselves of the stereotypes of single people as either objects of pity (because no one wanted to marry them) or objects of moral scorn (because they live such immoral lives) can we affirm the value that we find in this particular way of living in the world.

We have seen that at least in theory the Church has affirmed the value of the single lifestyle, while in practice it focused on religious vocations and the call to marriage, at least in the Church prior to the Second Vatican Council. The Council, which coincided with much political and social change in the "secular" world, had many insightful things to say about the people of God and their role in the world. If we look to the Council documents to see what they have to say about being single, what do we find?

For those of us in the United States, the source of our knowledge about what the Council Fathers said has been *The Documents of Vatican II*, edited by Walter Abbott. This book became a basic text among priests, religious and laity who wanted to know what the Council had been all about. When we read the documents of the Council, what do we find with reference to three states in life about which the Church has traditionally taught? The results are illuminating.

A cursory glance at the index to Abbott's volume yields thirty-nine references under the heading of "Marriage," with seven additional references to the rite of marriage and one additional reference each to the apostolate to married persons and their families and the family as a manifestation of Christian life. Priests receive one hundred references, in addition to five references to ordination and three to holy orders. Religious life has twenty references and religious orders, thirty-two, with another seventeen entries devoted to renewal in religious life. Vocations in general receive nine references, with another ten devoted to religious vocations in particular.

Single people? They receive one reference in particular. In *Lumen Gentium* (41), the Council Fathers speak of the role of bishops, priests, other ministers (such as deacons) and married couples. At the end of the paragraph devoted to married couples, the Council Fathers tell us, "A like example, but one given in a different way, is that offered by widows and single people, who are able to make great contributions toward holiness and apostolic endeavor in the Church."

Reading only one paragraph and the index to the Council documents can tell us a lot. Once again, the emphasis in the use of the word "vocation" lies in its connotation of a *religious* vocation. Sheer numbers of references tell us that the Council put priority on consideration of the priesthood. Yet another factor is of interest to us here, and that is the references to the rite of marriage and to ordination and the sacrament of holy orders. Both these states in life have a ritual dimension that is lacking for those called to the single state. Those called to the vowed life (who in a broad sense can be considered single) also have a ritual dimension in terms of profession ceremonies.

However, without looking at the Council documents we know from our experience that there is no ritual for singles. There have been pragmatic reasons for this: many people who are single have embraced that state in a transitory way, that is, they have been open to the possibility of being called to another state at a later point in life. Today we are becoming more aware of the importance of some type of rite that puts what we are doing into some kind of context. This is true, not just of sacramental rites, but also of ministries that do not involve sacramental ordination (lector, extraordinary minister of the Eucharist). We are also aware that just because a specific ritual does not exist, this does not mean that a particular moment in our lives is not in need of some type of public affirmation. One of the things that we have to examine, then, is the way in which single people can develop rituals that speak to significant events in their lives. Such rituals cannot be handed to single people from "on high;" they need to grow out of the experience of singles and reflect those moments in the single vocation that stand out as important. In this way, we draw on the richness of the single experience and the symbols which arise out of it.

As we consider all these possibilities, we stop and ask ourselves why being single is assuming prominence today in a way that is probably greater than at any other period in our culture. In America today there are 218 million Americans; 57 million of these are between 18–39 years of age. This is the largest population bloc in terms of numbers of any American sociology. Not only is this significant, but one half of those 57 million persons are single. We are becoming a single society. There are many reasons for any increasing number of single people in our society today. The divorce rate is soaring; many people are postponing marriage, especially women who are today pursuing higher education and careers in greater number. In the past a young person was more likely to live with his/her family until such time as he/she married, and this was logical in a day when most people were born, grew up and died in roughly the same geographical area. Today's increased mobility means that young people are more likely to move away from home to take advantage of an educational or career opportunity in another area of the country. Even those young people who continue their education or find a job in their home town are more likely to opt to live apart from their families. "Housing is seen as swinging to singles" was the headline of a *New York Daily News* article (December 25, 1978) that reported on a recommendation of the Citizens Housing and Planning Council. This civic group recommended that city officials concentrate on providing housing for what was termed "the city's fastest growing segment of the middle class population—singles, divorcees and couples without children." The council's director, Allan R. Talbot, went on to note that, although the total population of New York City is expected to drop between now and 1985, there will be a growth in the demand for housing due to an increase in one and two person households. This is typical of any large city or small community for that matter. Forty nine percent of all Americans live in one-person households.

One need only walk to the neighborhood newstand to note the proliferation of periodicals devoted to singles. An evening in front of the television provides a sample of weekly series that often have single people as the main characters, whether as individuals who have never married, or who find themselves single again through death or divorce. While we may judge some of these shows as having dubious social value, they are significant in that they are portraying people who are unmarried and who are not necessarily looking for a marriage partner in every episode. That television is portraying such situations is meaningful, since this medium often lags behind the social reality it seeks to present to its viewers. When the highly successful *Mary Tyler Moore Show* began several years ago, the original script called for the lead character to be a woman who relocated after a divorce. Some sentiment existed that this plot would be too "controversial," and thus Mary Richards appeared in Minneapolis as a result of a broken engagement. The show continued for several seasons, and the weekly plot more likely dealt with Mary's job and her relationship with co-workers and friends than it did with her search for a mate. The show ended and Mary was still single and eminently happy; that such a show was as successful in its day as *Father Knows Best* was some fifteen years before, tells us something about what viewers considered to be an accurate and acceptable portrayal of reality.

It almost belabors the obvious to point to the number of entertainment options designed especially for singles: bars, clubs, vacation plans and other get-togethers all compete for the time and money of single people. This, too, is a response to the growing number of single people who are looking for something to do and often have a healthy amount of money with which to do it. In the not too distant past, entertainment and vacations centered around the family and neighborhood, and economic necessities often precluded other possibilities. Here again, the increased mobility of our day means that many single people are living far from home and so do not look to the family for recreational activities. A high degree of specialization in social activities (separate activities for children, for adolescents, for parents) also contributes to a decline in family-centered or intergenerational activities. Our concept of neighborhood is changing too; mobility means that the make-up of any particular neighborhood changes very frequently. It is not uncommon for a young adult to make half a dozen major geographical moves in almost as many years. Part of this is due to a desire for career advancement which may necessitate relocating half a continent away. All of these factors are more prevalent today than ever before, and while they have many positive effects, they bring with them some negative aspects too. The family cannot be the support system it once was if the family is thousands of miles away, neighborhood does not mean what it once did if residents stay there a few years at most.

The description of singles, therefore, is different today than it was before, and the differences are significant. There are more single people, as we have noted, and the *nature* of what it means to be single is different. It does not necessarily mean living with or near one's family, and it means a variety of reasons for and ways of being single.

The high divorce rate has contributed to the increased number of single persons. A good percentage of divorced people will enter into another marriage and thus cease to be single, but some will never remarry. Especially among older adults, some will become single because of death of a spouse; some will remarry and some will not. Of the "never marrieds," some will eventually marry and some will remain single either through choice or chance. Included in those who never marry are those who live with another in a long-term relationship without either civil or ecclesiastical sanction. Homosexual persons are another subgroup of singles, some of whom may live in long-term relationships that cannot be sanctioned legally or ecclesiastically. The Council Fathers, as noted above, referred to "widows and single people;" they were only scratching the surface of the many ways of being single in today's world. Large numbers of persons are single in a very different way than our childhood experience of Aunt Alice and Uncle Phil.

There have always been single people in human history, and they have been single for any and all of the reasons we have noted above. We have looked at some of the reasons that make being single today different from being single at any other time in history. Sheer numbers have made singles more visible, and have caused various agents in society (for reasons ranging from the humanistic to the purely materialistic) to offer more and varied activities and products designed especially for singles. Where, in all of this, is the Church?

It is the perception and reality of many single people within the Church that the Church has offered little support or encouragement to singles. People with this outlook point to the resources (both monetary and personnel) that the Church pours into the education and socialization of children and adolescents; the number of adult programs which as a result of this emphasis on children are directed toward parents; the Church pronouncements, both official and local, on sexuality which do not speak to the experience of single adults; and, finally, the one class of unmarried people who receive a great deal of time and resources from the Church: clergy and religious. For many people, this lack of support and interest has been sufficient cause for severing all but the most tenuous ties with the official Church. And large numbers of singles have made that choice.

Of course we can point to signs of hope. There have been great strides in establishing programs on national, diocesan and local levels for single people. The growth of the divorced Catholics movement has met many of the needs of a particular group of single Catholics. Yet even these advances are not enough, and it is patronizing to recite a list of present accomplishments to a person who has not himself or herself experienced a sense of welcome in the Christian community.

One woman, for example, reflected on her own experience as a single adult in the Church. She is in her late forties, has a successful career in business and has been single all her life. She is active in her parish and is a generous contributor to parish needs. A real moment of pain came for her when the parish chose extraordinary ministers of the Eucharist, and no single persons were included. She herself had no desire to be an extraordinary minister, and in fact had gone through a period of genuine internal struggle before coming to accept the institution of this ministry. She could point to several single people in the parish who were persons of deep spirituality and who had given much to the parish over the course of many years. "I really feel that many single people give an awful lot to the Church," she said quietly, "but the Church just takes them for granted."

In spite of these feelings, this woman continues to take an active role in her parish, and the Church is fortunate for that. Before we dismiss her complaint as just one small issue we should stop to consider how many other "small" neglects of single people had brought her to this feeling of being taken for granted. And we have to stop and wonder how many other people have experienced these same feelings of neglect and being taken for granted, and who have opted to deal with the pain by withdrawing.

It is easy, and somewhat useless, to chastise the Church for its neglect of singles. It is more productive to look to the present and the future and examine what we can do to change our present course with regard to single people. As we have seen, the Church has always spoken about being single as a vocation, that is, a call from God. In practice, however, we have not claimed the single vocation as our own. We know very little about what it means to be single, especially in this latter half of the twentieth century, and because of this, we have a lot of listening to do. We need to listen to singles talk about their experience of being single, and we need to do this in a nonjudgmental way. The authorities on what it means to be single are not celibates or married people, but singles themselves. Singles are living the single life in a variety of ways, and living that life in fidelity to the gospel, with only minimal help from the institutional Church. It is time for the Church to learn about singles by studying what information is available about singleness in its many forms. And most of all, it is time to listen to the stories of single people, to hear what they are saying about the issues that are of importance in their lives, and to begin to respond to the challenge that single people offer the Church.

FOLLOW UP EXERCISES

Reflection

1. Think back to an important figure in your childhood who was single. Answer the following with regard to him or her. If possible, ask a single friend to answer these questions separately, and then share your reflections when both of you are finished.

Did he or she seem to be happily single?

Was any explanation ever offered as to why this person was single? If so, what was it?

What was my opinion of this person when I was a child?

What is my opinion now?

What influence has this person had on my life as a single person?

2. The following exercise can be done alone, or in a small group of single adults.

Imagine that you are working with a group of high school seniors who are having a day of discussion and reflection on lifestyles. Design the segment of the program that will deal with single life. Include:

• the positive value of being single
• important issues for single people
• models for single living (past, present, well known, local)

How does this exercise clarify your understanding of (a)aspects of single living that are most important to you; (b)the people who serve as your models for single living?

Is there any possibility of implementing this plan with a group of young people?

Prayer and Reflection
The following readings are sources of reflection that can be readily applied to the single life. Use them as sources for personal reflection, or let them serve as a starting point for the creation, with friends, of a ritual for single adults.

Jeremiah 1:4–8
Psalm 25:1–10
1 John 1:1–3
Ephesians 3:14–21
Romans 12:4–15
John 15:9–17

The following music may be used to complement your personal reflection or as part of a ritual.

St. Louis Jesuits: "Earthen Vessels" (album of the same name); "One Bread, One Body" and "Come to the Water" (*Wood Hath Hope*). Dameans: "All That We Have" (*Tell the World*). Weston Priory: "All I Ask of You" and "The Lord Jesus" (*Listen*).

Singles:
A
Look
at
the
Present

The media and our own experience may tell us that the young adult population, particularly the singles sub-group, is growing and changing. Yet, even with these perceptions it is helpful to have some hard data regarding this population group. While statistics are not infallible, they do help to give us a sense of what is happening across the country. What do statistics tell us about young adults, especially single young adults?

In the first place, the young adult population as a whole represents a large portion of the population of the United States. According to the U.S. Bureau of Census, there were 214,659,000 people living in the United States in 1976. Of these, 12,641,000 were between the ages of 18 and 20, and 70,194,000 were between the ages of 21 and 44. This latter group alone represents approximately one-third of the country's population. It also seems reasonable to estimate that this population is growing and will continue to grow for a period. High school enrollment in 1977 was up 7% from 1970, and during the same period, college enrollment increased by 38%. Interestingly, most of this increase took place among 25–34 year olds and among women.

Furthermore, the number of single people is also increasing. The number of women in their early twenties who were never married increased from 36% in 1970 to 45% in 1977. It is estimated that 38% of the first marriages of women now in their late twenties will end in divorce.

Naturally, an increase in the divorce rate will also cause an increase in the number of single people. In 1970, approximately one divorce occurred for every three marriages; in 1977, 2,176,000 marriages took place, while there were 1,097,000 divorces. Provisional figures for 1977 indicate that there are 10.1 married people per 1,000 population, with 5.0 divorced persons per 1,000 population. But while marriage may be suffering, heterosexual relationships of other kinds are growing: this decade has seen an 83% increase in the number of unrelated couples of the opposite sex who are living together.

The reason for the growth in the young adult population is easier to explain than is any other aspect of this shift. The 25- to 34-year old population has grown 32% since 1970, the result of the so-called "baby boom" that occurred after World War II. As the baby boom population grows up, the median age of the population shifts: in 1970 the median age was 27.9 years, compared with 29.4 in 1977. According to Manuel D. Plotkin, Director of the Census Bureau, there is an increasing proportion of young married women who are postponing childbearing: the number of women 20 to 24 years of age who had ever married, but were childless, increased from 36% in 1970 to 43% in 1977. The declining birthrate is reflected in declining enrollments in kindergartens and elementary schools. Although the birthrate rose slightly in 1977, it would seem that for a while, at least, it is the young adult population that will be predominant in the population. Even a cursory look at ads for various consumer goods indicates that advertisers are seeking to attract the attention of a population that is young but yet has the means to afford the latest in clothing, cars, stereo equipment, etc.—in short, the young adult population.

The statistics with regard to postponement of marriage and the increase in divorces point out that the number of single people of all ages is growing. It will be interesting to see how many of those who have "postponed" marriage, or who have ended a marriage, eventually marry or marry again. Among this population—those who will never marry and those who will divorce and never marry again—several key issues emerge. Unless and until the Church addresses these issues, its ministry to singles will have a hollow ring.

Many Ways of Being Single

There will always be a large number of people for whom being single will be a transistional state, occurring before marriage and perhaps between marriages. The majority of people will probably marry at some time in their lives. However, as we have seen, more people are postponing marriage, meaning that they will be single longer than might have been the case ten or twenty years ago. And there will be a growing number of people who will choose not to marry or remarry at all. Perhaps part of the reason that the Church has paid so little attention to singles in the past is that it seemed to be a state in life of short duration. Children will remain children for a fixed number of years, and married persons are married (or so it was hoped) for life. Here were two groups that had something of a stable population and a somewhat predictable set of needs and developmental tasks. For single young adults, however, this is not the case. Even though each child is unique and each marriage is unique, there are many common needs and traits within each group. Part of the failure of some of the programs designed by the Church for singles has been the assumption that singles are a heterogenous group. And the assumption generally was that the common thread that held singles together was their desire to get married.

The Church in our day is faced with the realization—brought home to it by the media, if not by its own members—that being single takes many different forms. It can mean never having been married, or having been married and then "singled" through death or divorce. It can mean being single at twenty-two, perhaps still in school and living at home with family, or it can mean being single at thirty-five, established in a job and living in one's own home. It can mean being a single man, faced with the societal pressures of living as a "swinging bachelor," or it can mean being a single woman, faced with the societal pressure of "catching" someone. It can mean being single by choice or by chance. It can mean, as it will for a majority of people, being single as a transitional state, or it can mean, as it will for a growing number, being single permanently. Faced with the variety of ways of being single, and the multitude of special needs and issues that come with that variety, it is perhaps not surprising that the Church has seemed so reluctant to address the single population. It may even seem to be wiser to leave such a complex issue alone. However, that wisdom is quickly being replaced by the recognition that the Church is ignoring a growing number of its members—or former members. Before the Church attempts to speak with single adults, it needs to learn more about them. In Chapter Three, we will look at some of the basic information about single people that the Church needs to assimilate before it can begin a viable ministry to single adults.

Intimacy and Relationships

The paramount issue in human life is that of relationships. It seems dangerous to make an absolute statement about human existence, but it cannot be denied that we are societal creatures for whom relationships with others—parents, siblings, friends, spouses, children, God— are of utmost importance. This is certainly true of single people. Like anyone else, the single person must relate to family, neighbors, friends, co-workers, passing acquaintances. Perhaps more so than married people and those who live in the structure of a religious community, the single person is in need of quality, supportive, intimate relationships that complement the single life that he or she is living. Single people are often referred to as "unattached;" while it is true that they are not married, they are very much attached to a variety of other people, and improving and maintaining these relationships are important.

While familial relationships and friendships are important to the single person, single people are also concerned with romantic or sexual relationships. For single people who plan to marry or marry again, such relationships are important because any given relationship may be the one that develops into a commitment that can last for a lifetime. Developing and maintaining an intimate relationship with another person is hard work. We have only to look at some of the forces working against such a relatiońship to know just how difficult it is. Novels, magazine articles, movies, and songs often emphasize the positive points of temporary liaisons, while giving far less attention to relationships that endure beyond this week, this month, or even this evening. The rising divorce rate shows that even when people enter into a relationship with the best of intentions, determined to make things "work," it is difficult to make such a relationship life-long and vital.

Whether or not a single person enters into a particular relationships with the idea or hope that it might lead to marriage, there are questions and concerns about developing the relationship so that it is a growing one for both persons involved. A single person who is in his or her twenties or thirties is not in the same situation as a high school student who is beginning to date. Although this is so obvious as to be trite, it is not always obvious to those who claim to speak for the Church about relationships, párticularly the sexual aspect of relationships. As Church, we sometimes tend to spcak to adults as if they were children. We ignore what we don't want to know, hoping that in the process the truth will go away.

I spoke recently to a priest who does some counseling work with men entering religious orders. He was somewhat disturbed by some of the formation programs he had observed: "Twenty years ago or so," he said, "the vast majority of candidates for religious life were right out of high school. Essentially, we were preparing virgins to live a life of celibacy, and a particular type of formation and counseling arose from that. Today, we're talking about men who have gone to college, held jobs, dated, perhaps even lived with someone for a period of time. So, we're talking about preparing men for a celibate life who have had some amount of sexual experience. The formation has to be different. But no one wants to talk about that, so we keep doing the same old thing."

The point that the priest was making is an equally valid one when we are talking about single adults and their sexual experience. It is of no help to anyone to talk to single adults about sex as if their experience in that area was nonexistent. This is especially true when we think of the number of single people who have been previously married. The Church upholds an ideal about sexual expression, and it is an important ideal, however, upholding the ideal is not synonymous with refusing to admit that not everyone is living the ideal.

Intimacy is a central issue for single adults. It is the road on which we travel, not some destination that we reach once and for all. In Chapter Four, we will examine some key points of the intimacy issue, and how the Church can speak to single adults on this issue.

Meaningful Work

In a much earlier age than this one, work was a rather simple issue. When people made their living from the fruit of their own labor, it was important for people to have large families to provide a labor force for the family farm. In the Old Testament, which gives us a slice of the history of a very early age, we find numerous stories of people who lived off whatever the land produced. A similar system of "making a living" more or less held true until the industrial revolution. One does not have to be an expert in the writings of Karl Marx to know that the coming of the industrial age and capitalism produced an unprecedented change in the kind of work one could do and the ways in which one could make a living.

Today in our country it is still possible to make one's living from farming—although the farm of today is vastly different from the farm of earlier ages. However, the vast majority of people in the United States today make their living at other than agricultural jobs. The variety of jobs is astounding, as is the compensation. To get an idea of the extremes, one only has to think of an unskilled laborer who is making the minimum wage (less than three dollars an hour in 1979), who is watching a baseball game in which the team's star player, [who is trying to hit a ball over a fence,] is paid perhaps close to a million dollars a year to work from April to September. Work, its nature, and its compensation obviously are complex issues that deserve some consideration.

Even if one is not a professional athlete, it is possible to make what is considered a high salary in this country. Such a salary enables a person to lead "the good life" and to acquire many of the goods that advertisers tell us are necessary for our happiness. Yet a large wage does not mean that other aspects of a job are equally attractive. I remember talking to a young man who was making a good salary working with computers. He and his wife had three children, and his salary enabled them to own their own home, afford a nice vacation every year, send the older children to Catholic schools, and still save some money every year. It was his wife's wish to be at home with the children while they were growing up, and his salary made that possible. The only problem in this otherwise idyllic situation was that he hated his job. He was good at it, but disliked the nature of his work and the pressure that sometimes came with it. He had dropped out of college after his first year, but had held onto the desire to be a research biologist. At this point, the possibility of getting a less demanding (and lower paying) job so that he could go back to school seemed out of the question. Even if his wife went back to work, she would not be able to earn much since she had been out of the labor force for ten years. He enjoyed his lifestyle, but disliked the means by which he and his family were able to live it.

It might seem difficult to feel sorry for someone with a high-paying job, but the young man in question points up the fact that there is not always a direct relationship between what we are paid for a job, and the nature of the work and the satisfaction it brings us. Even as many people are able to achieve unparalleled affluence (a goal which we are so often told is to be devoutly desired), there still remains the question of the price that is paid for such affluence in non-monetary terms. For what am I being paid? Is what I accomplish making a positive contribution to the society in which I live? Is it giving me a sense of satisfaction? As more people find affluence within their reach, the work issue for them will change from a question of just wage for a day's work to a consideration of the nature of the work they are doing and the effect it is having on them as persons.

In the same country in which such affluence is a real possibility for some, poverty is the reality for others. Such poverty can result from low-paying jobs, or it may be caused by not being able to get a job at all. According to the Bureau of Labor Statistics, in May, 1978, those hardest hit by unemployment were the young. Persons of both sexes aged sixteen to nineteen had an unemployment rate of 16.5%. For non-Whites, this percentage jumped to 38.4. In 1976, 12% of the population lived in poverty, the largest percentage of this group being families of female householders with no husband present. At the same time, the total number of households headed by women with no husband present increased from 5.7 million in 1970 to 7.9 million in 1977. Unemployment and poverty are problems that plague young adults, particularly those among minorities, and single women who are raising families.

At the same time, the number of women in the labor force is growing. Women constituted 41% of the civilian labor force in 1977, and accounted for 57% of the increase in the civilian labor force in the first seven years of this decade. As more opportunities open up for women in professional and related fields, we see an increase in the number of women who hold jobs that were once almost the exclusive domain of men: there was an increase of 867,000 women in professional and related fields in the period of 1975-77 alone. Women, then, are gaining more and more opportunities for the affluence we mentioned earlier, but they are also most heavily affected by the consequences of poverty.

For a growing number of lay people, including and especially single lay people, work means work within the Church in some form of ministry. Here the issues of affluence that come from a high-paying job are not prominent. The question is rather that of just wages and benefits within the Church itself. The Church, which has had so many prophetic things to say about just wages, often finds itself in the embarrassing position of paying those in its employ a less than living wage. Often single people are able to stay in Church work because they are the only ones who can even consider living on a Church salary. All of us have probably had the experience of knowing someone who gave up a ministerial job—one for which the person had great aptitude and great love—because he or she married and had to think of the practical realities of supporting a family. To such people, the phrase "poor as church mice" is not merely a throwback to another era.

For those who stay in ministerial work, either despite the salary or because he or she is fortunate enough to be receiving a living wage, there are other problems. Too many people still equate ministry with ordination. The lay person on the team is not as "equal" as his or her clerical colleagues. This is especially true for women, who in the pecking order are often less equal than the laymen. Lay persons often learn that pursuing one's education in theology or religious education or a related field does not necessarily mean advancement, either in terms of salary or responsibility: the real power lies with those who wear the collar.

It should not surprise us, then, that lay people who pursue careers in ministry do not often stay there long. It usually has little to do with their dedication or their desire to be lay ministers. The truth is that we are losing some of our best lay people because we are not paying them a living wage, we are not willing to give them positions of responsibility—in short, we are not willing to validate their ministry as an authentic one. Many people who might be interested in pursing careers in ministry see themselves being invited to find a subordinate place in the clerical caste system. They see themselves as being invited to buy one of the remaining tickets to the *Titanic* and, not surprisingly, many politely decline.

Work is a central issue for single adults, whether they are working in the business world or within the Church itself. In Chapter Five we will expand on some of the problems that are work-related, and examine the way in which the Church can speak and act with credibility on these issues.

A Believing Community

As important as all of the issues discussed above are, at the heart of the matter is the attitude of the Church itself toward single adults. The Church will only be able to speak authentically and with feeling to the issues we have described when and if the Church affirms the importance of the single adult population. This affirmation has to take place through more than words, although words are important. The Church must show through words and deeds that it has a commitment to single adults.

Four important issues emerge when we discuss the Church's relationship to single adults. We will examine them briefly here, and look at them in more depth in Chapter Six.

1. *Evangelization.* We hear a lot in the Church today about evangelization. One particular thrust of evangelization is the attempt to speak to those who no longer feel that they are part of the Church community. People have dissaffiliated from the Church for a variety of reasons. Of concern to us here is the number of single and young adults who no longer consider themselves part of the Church community. Obviously, not all of them will want to re-establish their ties with the Roman Catholic community. Regardless of this, the Church needs to learn and understand the reasons why some single adults feel alienated from the Church. This understanding will only come about if the Church actively *listens* to what single adults are saying. The evangelization process must be one of listening, and not just of programs.

2. *Adult Catechesis.* Read the course offerings of any college in the country today, and you are bound to read of many courses that are designed for adults who wish to continue learning after their formal education has ended. As Church, we can learn a powerful lesson from the secular world. It is essential that we provide adult Catholics with the opportunity to learn about and grow in their faith during their adult years. In the past, we have worked under the mistaken notion that it was necessary (and sufficient) to teach children and adolescents

everything about the faith by the time they finished high school. We will provide a great service to our young people if we recognize that we cannot "give" them everything they need to know by a prescribed age. We will provide an even greater opportunity to people of all ages if we recognize that learning about the faith, sharing it with others, and growing in an appreciation of it is a process that lasts a lifetime.

3. *Lay Single Leadership.* We have touched on the fact that more and more frequently we are finding lay people in positions of leadership within the Church. The opportunities for such leadership and an understanding of the nature of such leadership are crucial if lay people are to have a real voice within the Church. Part of affirming the place of single adults within the Church will be fostering the leadership skills and talents that single people possess. Single adults must know that the leadership they are being called to is a graced opportunity and a challenge, not merely an occasion for further frustration.

4. *Singles Speak to the Church.* So far, we have concentrated on the Church's "reaching out" to single adults. Even as we speak of this, it is important to remember that single adults are also speaking to the Church. It is not the case that "we" are Church and "they" are outside of it (in theory or in fact.) Single adults are creating Church wherever they are; sometimes it is in an institutional setting and sometimes it is not. The community that exists where single young adults gather is calling and challenging the Church. Even as the Church attempts to speak to single adults about topics that are of relevance to them, the Church must be listening to the voices of the single people in its midst.

The Church is called in every age to respond to unique problems and needs. Like any human institution, the Church can look back with pride on those moments when it has responded with vision and courage, and with sorrow on those moments when it has failed to read correctly the signs of the times. There are many pressing issues that face the Church today, and one of them is the Church's response to single adults. We have seen how the size and nature of the single and young adult population has changed and is changing. We know from our own experience that many institutions within our society are responding to those changes—and not always in the most positive way. The question that remains to be answered is how the Church will respond.

FOLLOW UP EXERCISES

1. Assess the "facts" of your singleness.
   Age_____
   Sex_____
   Occupation _____
   1. I (a)have always been single; (b)am single because of divorce or separation; (c)am single because of death of a spouse.
   2. I live (a)with my family; (b)alone; (c) _____.
   3. At this point in my life, I consider my singleness (a)transitional; (b)permanent; (c)not sure.
      Why? _____
   4. At this point in my life, I view being single as (a)my conscious choice; (b)a matter of circumstance.
      Why? _____

Complete these questions on your own and share with a friend or group of friends who have also done this exercise. What difference do factors such as age, sex, living arrangements, etc., make in being single?

2. Of the issues identified as primary for single adults, which are most important to you? Rank the following and describe for each issue the specific aspect that you feel is a concern in your life now.

Rank   *Issue*   *Specific Concern*
         Intimacy/Relationships
         Work
         Faith community
         Adult catechesis
         Lay single leadership in Church

What is my #1 concern? In the last three months, what have I done concretely to further my growth in this aspect of my life?

Prayer and Reflection

1. How can I appreciate more the uniqueness that is part of each person?

2. How much of my life is a matter of accepting circumstances rather than shaping them when and where I can? Identify one current issue

where circumstances are shaping *you*. Decide on one concrete step that can be taken to change this.

3. Read Matthew 5:43–48. How would you translate "perfect"? Does it mean "having it all together"? If not, how would you describe it?

Many Ways to Be Single

Universal terms are essential to thought and communication, and it is difficult to see how we would conduct our daily lives if we had to think up a new name for every object that we came across. The problem with universal terms, as they apply to people, is that they begin to collect sets of characteristics around them, and in time these characteristics can become accepted as truth. Such generalizations may be complementary ("I'm so glad we hired a couple of young people. They're always so full of fresh ideas.") or they may be derogatory ("I don't let my girlfriend do anything with the car except drive it. You know what poor mechanics women are."). As we broaden our personal experience we learn that the truth of such statements is determined by an individual's make-up, and not by inherent traits of a particular group. (Some young people are extremely unimaginative and some women are good mechanics.) If a trait *seems* to hold true of an entire group, we find that cultural and historical conditions have contributed heavily to this. Ten or more years ago, no woman was encouraged or given the opportunity to learn about the workings of a car; today, this is changing. We do know that stereotypes are dangerous because they lead us to false assumptions about individuals and groups, and because they prevent us from seeing a whole range of human experience.

As single people become more numerous and more prominent in our society, these same dangers of stereotyping become prevalent. We need to examine some of the myths of singleness that are beginning to surface. It is important to note here the use of the word "myth." This term is often used to denote a story, which, while not true in its literal sense, helps us to understand reality in a deeper way. I am using the word "myth" in its more common, everyday usage, to denote a statement or story that describes reality in a way that is fundamentally at odds with the facts.

We saw in Chapter One some of the derogatory ways in which the word "single" is often used. Let's look now at some of the characteristics or qualities of singleness that are erroneous descriptions of the single state.

Anyone can be single.
We saw earlier that there is a lack of ritual dimension for the single state. Because the commitment of a married couple or a vowed religious is announced and celebrated in some type of public ceremony, we have a tangible sign of that commitment. Because the same thing is not true of being single, we do not think of being single as a decisive act. While

getting married in our culture has a more or less set pattern of events (meeting another, getting to know him/her, falling in love, announcing the engagement, marrying), and religious life also has its unique process of commitment (entrance into a community, a novitiate period, vows), being single does not have such a visible process (although there may be and usually is a very definite internal one). And while there are some people who live and die without ever marrying, and others who live and die without ever joining a religious community, there is no one who dies without being single. All of these factors have contributed to a sense that being single is something that anyone can do. It requires no decision, is not a commitment of any kind, and requires little talent other than the ability to breathe.

A few years ago I read an interview with a female entertainer. Her marriage had ended a couple of years before, and she immediately began living with another man. That relationship had ended shortly before the interview took place, and she remarked with some shock to the interviewer, "This is the first time in twelve years that I haven't been in some kind of heavy relationship with a man!" Her statement reminded me of the days when I worked with college students. There were always a few people (of either sex) who were constantly involved with someone. I asked one young woman who was in a relationship that had clearly lost all its positive value why she didn't break up with her boyfriend. "Oh, we won't split up until I'm sure I have someone else."

Obviously some people need to be part of a twosome. Their statements may indicate that they prefer to be part of a couple because it is more fun or more fulfilling to have a significant other in their lives. But I wonder if such a stance toward being alone indicates some sense that living outside a permanent relationship (or one as permanent as two people may define it) requires skills and strengths that not everyone has at all moments of his or her life.

The young woman I spoke of seemed to see being unattached as something to be avoided at all costs. I am not suggesting that all people who marry do so to avoid being single. By the same token, we should not assume that all people who are single have avoided marriage, either because of lack of ability to "find someone" or lack of skill in relating to others.

Remember when you first learned to ride a bicycle or jump rope or dive off the high board? Mastering the challenge brought tremendous feelings of pride and achievement with it. Perhaps an older boy or girl was watching as you performed, and then remarked, "Oh, *anyone* can do that." And suddenly the very special accomplishment wasn't so special any more.

When we believe that anyone can do something, we negate the value of that act to a great degree. We know that not everyone is called to marriage or religious life, and we value the witness that these states in life give to us. As soon as we begin to understand that not everyone is called to be single, that being single requires special gifts, just as marriage and religious life do, then we will begin to value the single state and the people who live it. Only then will we appreciate the unique witness that single people have to give us.

Being single is a matter of not being something else.
We saw in Chapter One that we often use terms such as "unmarried" and "premarital" to refer to various aspects of the single state. Such terminology defines one state in terms of another, and is another factor in negating the value of being single. We don't refer to married people as "unsingle" and perhaps it is time to do single people the service of retiring such words as "unmarried" once and for all.

If, as we have said, being single is a unique call that requires unique gifts and gives a unique witness to the Church and the world, then being single has a value that is independent of others states in life. It deserves to be spoken of on its own terms, and those terms are positive ones. When we begin to speak of single people in such positive terms, we will be on the road to admitting that being single brings its own kind of fulfillment, and is not merely a lack of something else.

Being single is a unilateral experience.
The myths that fall under this category are numerous, and it is best to examine them by kind.

Age.
Work in the field of the stages of adult life are making us more aware of the fact that different periods of adulthood have specific tasks and specific concerns. If this is true of adulthood in general, it is certainly true of single adulthood. A look at two brief stories will help to illustrate this.

Mary graduated from college with a degree in education and began teaching elementary school. She found herself becoming more interested in her "problem" students, most of whom, she learned, came from families with a history of problems (alcoholism, physical abuse, unemployment). She continued to teach but studied evenings and summers for a Masters degree in counseling. After she received her degree, she realized that her own desire for better training, plus the heavy competition for jobs in the field of psychology, would necessitate her getting a Ph.D. She received a fellowship to study at a university with a good program in child development. The university was several hundred miles away from her home, which meant living away from her parents and family for the first time in her life. Mary felt that the experience of being on her own was important, and so she regarded the move as an additional benefit of her decision to study. At twenty-nine, Mary is just finishing her Ph.D. and has been hired to work in a child counseling center. Although her new job is within commuting distance of her parents' home, she intends to rent her own apartment. She has an educational loan to pay off, but is confident that she can be rid of her debts in a few years. Her immediate goal is to get a few years' experience at the center and perhaps meet a few other psychologists who share her dream of establishing a private practice where she can do play therapy with disturbed children. Although Mary enjoys working with children tremendously, she more and more doubts that she herself wishes to be a parent. She is seriously considering postponing marriage until her late thirties when her practice is established. Since she doesn't think she wants children, she feels that the age at which she marries—if she marries at all—is immaterial.

Lois is also a teacher. She is in her early fifties and has been a high school English teacher since her graduation from college. Like Mary, she studied part time for her Master's degree. She began working toward a Ph.D. but discontinued her studies because of lack of interest and the fact that her job did not require an advanced degree. Lois is single and up until five years ago lived all her life with her parents. Her mother died in a car accident seven years ago, and her father, who had already been an invalid for several years due to a series of strokes, died two years later. Much of Lois' free time in those two years after her mother's death was consumed in caring for her father. Now that she is alone in the house and does not have to invest her time in the care of her father, she finds herself feeling lonely in a way that she never did before. Lois does not regret not having married, for her career has been satisfying and she feels she had the kind of friendships and social activities that she wanted. She has kept in touch with several old friends who have married, and saw them frequently when their children were grown but did not yet have families of their own. Now that her friends are becoming grandparents, they invest more of their time in their children and grandchildren. Some have begun to move to adult communities in others states. Lois has thought about doing that also, but a move would mean changing jobs. She has also considered returning to school to get her Ph.D. so that she could teach in a college, but the idea of beginning anew in a more competitive atmosphere frightens her. As she gets older she feels that her options are more limited than they were ten or twenty years ago. Her greatest fear is that she will become an invalid like her father was, for she worries that with no one to care for her she will wind up among strangers in a nursing home. More immediately, she is concerned about how to use her spare time in a fulfilling and useful way.

Mary and Lois represent in many ways two extremes and two very different attitudes. Mary has a good deal of her life ahead of her and is full of plans for the future; Lois reflects on how the choices she has made have determined her present situation, and her thoughts of the future are worrisome ones. Yet their attitudes are also very realistic ones. Mary feels that a whole world has opened up to her, and indeed it has; she is at the point where she is making her decisions and her options and power seem unlimited. *She* can decide on the direction she wishes her career to take; *she* can decide if she wants children. Surrounded as she is by people near to her in age and aspirations, Mary cannot be expected to think ahead to a time when her friends will move away or die. Much less can she be expected to consider what her life will be like when she is older and living with decisions rather than making them.

Of course, there are some young people who do not view their futures with the same kind of optimism that Mary does. Mary has been fortunate to be able to pursue her educational and career desires without economic or family responsibilities to modify her plans. Likewise, many older people view retirement as a time to pursue activities that they did not have time for while they were working. Yet we can see that there is a difference in being single early and later in life. The younger single person often sees life more in terms of what lies ahead. Possibilities seem greater, and one has more of a chance of being surrounded by peers who can act as a support system. In our culture, the process of growing older often accentuates one's aloneness and the fact that one's major life decisions have been made. On the positive side, we can see that the older single person experiences emotional ties that have lasted the course of a lifetime, and can look back with satisfaction on what has gone before. In any event, the needs and experiences of the single person change as he/she grows older.

Never married/formerly married.

While being single does have common experiences, there are differences between being single for all of one's life, and becoming single again after having been married. Any major life change demands adjustment. The person who has been single for all his adult life has most likely established a style of living and a support system that enhances his/her life. To find oneself single again can be a shock to the system, particularly if this new-found singleness is not the result of one's own choice, as with the death of a spouse or a divorce that was initiated by one's partner.

Just as there are myths about single people, there is a particular set of myths that surround those who are single again, especially in the case of those who are divorced. These include the idea that the newly single are eager to find another marriage partner. Many newly single people discover that friends are diligently arranging meetings with "eligible" men and women, when the person is question is hardly over the shock of the divorce or death that occasioned the new state in life. Even more destructive is the myth that divorced persons, particularly women, are "easy" sexual targets. In general, the newly single find themselves thrown into an entirely new life situation, which may include assuming new financial responsibilities and raising children alone. In the midst of these practical concerns, they must learn to live alone when for ten or twenty or thirty years they have been accustomed to sharing their lives with another person. We can see that many of the needs of the formerly married, particularly in the initial period of adjustment, are quite different from the needs of people who have been single all their lives.

Single by choice and single by chance.

Even though we have been stressing the positive value of being single and its worth as a state in life apart from being married, our experience tells us that there are single people who have remained single even though they want to get married. There are a variety of reasons for this, which range from the oft-quoted "The right one never came along," to more specific reasons, such as family obligations that have curtailed one's social life and prevented one from meeting potential marriage partners. Sometimes inertia sets in, as with the man who described his singleness by saying, "When I was younger there were lots of eligible women around, and I just put off making a decision. And then, all of a sudden, it seemed that the eligible women had disappeared." We might be tempted to tell such a person that there are organizations to join and activities to get involved with that will bring him into contact with women who might be desirable marriage partners. But the fact remains that a particular person's unique circumstances and personality traits often make such advice easier to give than to follow.

There is a vast difference between doing something because one chooses to do it, and doing it because no other alternative presents itself. People who are single by a decisive act of the will react differently to their singleness than do people who feel that their singleness was not their first choice. As one grows older, one may have established a satisfactory lifestyle and have lost much of the desire to marry. Yet such a person may look back to past opportunities and regret not having married earlier in life. The "answer" at this point in life may not necessarily be to "marry the person off" but to help him or her see the value of the life that they are living.

Gender.

Men and women experience singleness differently. Some of the reasons for this are cultural; some are biological in origin.

a. *Cultural.* Our society tends to place a greater social value on a single man than on a single woman. This seems to have its roots on the traditional dictum that men do the proposing and women do the accepting. A single man, especially one considered to be in the "prime" of his life, is often regarded as someone who has eluded capture, who has not been sufficiently charmed or enchanted by a woman so that he has decided to commit himself to her. A single woman, on the other hand, may be regarded as single because no one has asked her to marry him; *she* does not have whatever it takes to attract and keep a man. Mercifully, this attitude is changing, but significant traces of its still remain. This mindset is summed up in the question asked of bright, personable, attractive women who are single, a question often asked with a genuine air of surprise, "Why isn't a nice girl like you married?"

This entire situation is further complicated by the tradition that in any pairing the man is the same age or older than the woman. While there are exceptions to this, it tends to be the norm. Therefore a man's marriage prospects are never seen as diminishing, since more females

37

are always growing up and entering the adult population. Conversely, a woman's chances to meet a suitable mate are seen as decreasing as she grows older.

What effect does all of this have on being single? It tends to make the experience more difficult for a woman than for a man because she has societal pressures to cope with. It is often stated that if we hear something often enough we come to believe it. If women are told often enough that it is not a good thing to be a single woman, this will have an effect on a woman's self-image. The effects can be even more far-reaching. A former student of mine once related the story of his sister's marriage, which produced four children, much quarreling, and a painful divorce after ten years of marriage. The student said he was not surprised that the marriage finally ended; his sister had once confided to him that her prime motive for marrying had been that she was twenty-five when her husband proposed to her, and she did not think another chance for marriage would come along. Obviously her insecurities were part of her own make-up, but in a society that overemphasizes the attractiveness of youth and the value of proving one's worth by finding a partner. Such insecurities are nurtured.

There is one area in which cultural misinterpretations do not favor men, and that is in the area of sexual identity. A man who has never beer married, particularly as he grows older, may be subject to speculation regarding his heterosexuality. Witness the campaign of Edward Koch, who ran successfully for the office of Mayor of New York City in 1977. During that campaign, rumors circulated that he was a homosexual, the apparent reason for the stories being that some voters who would otherwise lean toward Koch would not vote for him if they believed he were gay. The sole basis for the rumors was the fact that Koch, who is in his fifties, has never been married.

Experience and statistics tell us that not all single people are homosexuals and not all married people are heterosexuals. Our society, with its history of defining masculinity so rigidly, has been more concerned with condemning male homosexuality than with condemning the same orientation in women. Hence it is more common for a man's masculine identity to be equated with his sexual preferences.

The element that these cultural stereotypes for single men and women have in common goes deeper than the myths of what makes a woman desirable and what makes a man masculine. The commonality lies in the misconception that there must be an explanation for singleness, and the explanation is not "good." To say a woman is single because no one wants her, or that a man is single because he is gay is in our society at the present time to make negative statements.

When people marry or enter religious life, we generally focus on the positive reasons for the decision. Even when circumstances might indicate otherwise (e.g., a materialistic person marries a rich spouse), we try to give people the benefit of the doubt. At the very least, we ought to do the same for single people. There are good, positive, healthy reasons for remaining single. We need to accept that, rather than search for an explanation that fits into our misconceptions about the single state.

b. *Biological.* "Biology is not destiny," has been one of the rallying cries of the women's movement, and it is true that roles should not be determined on the simple basis of a person's gender. We have shown that in many ways being single is a different experience for men than it is for women, and the differences we've talked about have been influenced by culture. But biology does play a role in one area. One of the questions that almost all adults consider at some point in their lives is the question of parenthood. It's a complex question for everyone, including singles. The growing number of states and child care agencies that look favorably on single parent adoptions means that single people who wish to be parents but do not wish to marry can do so through adoption. For those who are transitional singles (see below), the question of parenting affects their plans for marriage. This is particularly true of women. Consider Denise, a college administrator in her mid-thirties.

"I wish marriage could be considered independently of having children, but that's difficult to do. I'd like to get married, and am now seriously involved with a man. I think we'll eventually get married, but we still have some things to work out. I wouldn't want to become pregnant until a year or two after we marry, because I think a couple needs time to adjust to each other and to being married before they adjust to a baby. But I have to be realistic. I'm thirty-six, and my childbearing years are limited. I've read all the stories about the problems that can arise from pregnancies in one's late thirties or early forties. But I don't want to feel I'm rushing down the aisle just so I can have a baby."

John is the same age as Denise. He works for a construction company and has enjoyed being single.

"I never thought much about getting married. I liked being single and saw what marriage had done to some of my friends, both male and female. I love kids but sort of assumed I'd never have any. When

I met Carol and fell in love with her, I began to see that my marriage didn't have to be like those of my friends. Carol and I are going to be married next year. After that, we're both going to work for a few years so that we can save some money. Then we're going to start our family. We'd like to have three or four kids."

John can afford the luxury of waiting a few years to have children, because his fiance is twenty-four. We have only to think of the famous personalities we read of who father children later in life—Charlie Chaplin, John Wayne and Cary Grant come to mind—to know that for men age is not the crucial issue in childbearing that it is for women.

A second factor that is gender-related is the life expectancy of adults in the United States, which is presently higher for women than it is for men. At present, statistics indicate that three out of four women will outlive their husbands. This means that the majority of people becoming single again because of death of a spouse will be women. This has several implications:

1. Women who wish to marry again find fewer opportunities to do so.

2. Women whose income was previously only part of a family's economic resources now find themselves the sole support of themselves and/or their children.

3. Women who left the job market to be full-time homemakers may now find themselves forced to reenter the job market—a market which is increasingly competitive and which may be overwhelming to a woman whose professional skills have not been used for a significant period of time.

4. Women who must rely on Social Security or some form of public assistance must adjust to the vagaries of a fixed income.

Merely from an economic point of view, the experience of a single woman can differ drastically from that of a single man. Even among women themselves, the economic situation of a newly single woman may be very different from that of a woman who has worked outside the home all of her adult life.

Transitional Singles/Permanent Singles.
As has been noted in many of our considerations, some single people are single for their entire lives and some become single again after being

married for a period. We have already considered some of the special concerns of people who become single after their marriage has ended. Especially for younger adults who are single, the single state may be looked upon as a transitional period that will end when they meet a suitable mate and decide to marry. For such singles, the period of being single may be marked by such goals as education, beginning careers, changing careers, relocating geographically (perhaps several times) and forming relationships. This latter might include living with a member of the opposite sex for a period of time.

While being single may sound very exciting, it brings with it an attendant set of problems. Education is expensive and time-consuming. The job market is tight and unemployment is a problem, particularly for certain segments of the population, such as young adult Black males. Housing, especially in large cities, is difficult to come by and expensive when found. Opportunities for meeting people may take the form of bars, dances, etc., that can exploit people both financially and emotionally. The pressure to marry, which can be external as well as internal, can be overwhelming. Loneliness, which is a component of everyone's life, can be felt more deeply when one is living alone, or living in a strange city, or unemployed, or faced with financial problems.

All of these problems are very real, and when we add to them the various myths which we have examined regarding singles, we can see that being single is a difficult experience at times. It further seems that the great interest in singles currently being exhibited by some sectors of society is based on a desire to fill the perceived vacuum in the lives of singles, and reap whatever monetary rewards are to be garnered. It is in the midst of this that the Church stands, faced with the decision about what its role will be in the lives of singles. The answer will depend very much on how the Church sees the question. Are we asking ourselves what singles "need" from us to get their lives in order, or are we asking how one part of the Church (the institution and its representatives) can join in ministry with another part of the Church (singles)? To ask the first question is to invite the perceived failure of the kinds of outreach to singles that have not worked in the past. To ask the second question is to open ourselves to the possibility of replies that we have never dreamed of.

Consider the case of the following single young adult, a man in his early thirties. He's poor and considered part of a subservient group by the people who rule his country. He has little formal education and a skill that barely supports him. The predominant pattern among his people is to grow up, get married, have a family, and earn whatever one can with one's skill. Don't rock the boat. Don't ask questions. But he did, and the rest is quite literally history.

It's easy to recognize Jesus of Nazareth in the preceding description. His story is well-known—perhaps too well-known, in a sense—to all of us. But until we learn to recognize the story of Jesus in the stories of single people, we have not really learned what his story was all about.

FOLLOW UP EXERCISES

1. What stereotypes that are attached to singles do you find most offensive? Why?

2. Which of the myths described here has been most harmful to you? What can you do to help eliminate this myth?

3. The word *myth*, when used in its more proper, precise meaning, refers to a story that helps us to *understand better* a particular reality. With a group of friends, do the following:
- lists movies, plays, stories, TV shows, etc., that give realistic portrayals of single people in our society
- discuss what elements of these media pieces contribute to their realism
- together, create an outline for a show, play, etc., that you feel would help to contribute to a better understanding of being single.

Prayer and Reflection
1. Read the Magnificat (Luke 1:46–55). Reflect on it and write a magnificat for single people. Share it with friends and ask their reactions.

2. Jesus was a single person living in a predominantly married society. As an ongoing process of reflection for yourself, do the following:

- pick one gospel (Mark is the shortest) and read a section of it each day
- after each reading, reflect on:
  the problems that Jesus faced as a single person
  what a particular incident or scene offers single people as a model for their own lives.

Singles:
Intimacy
and
Relationships

If we take seriously the reality that God became human, that is, that divinity can be expressed fittingly in human terms, then we have to take the history of our human family in light of what it means to be made in God's image and likeness. God is eternal, yet we know him only in the stories of the history of millions of people who walked the incarnational journey and called themselves Christian. Humans are people of historical background; they have very important stories, individually and collectively. The human family is like a great tapestry of thousands and thousands of years in which we take a very important part in weaving our own humanness and spiritual search.

Only when we step back and take a larger picture of the histories of peoples do we come by a manageable grasp of a very powerful lesson in creation history. God has provided for each of us, not in an anonymous way, but in a specific way in relating us to one another. In the Old Testament there is very careful detail on dozens of occasions in relating one family to another in a whole lineage. These blood relationships identify families and individuals, and more importantly, show the hand of God's love as a primary example of how we are to be with one another and to care for one another. Our existence goes beyond just an individual identity. Jesus is the linking point that networks the emphasis of the Old Testament. Simply speaking of identity in terms of family and Yahweh's people with Jesus' life, we begin to build on that, go beyond it, and claim a new identity as Christians. Christ enters history in a bodily form and lives a simple life of intimate relationships for 30 years with family and friends. This reality is to be our model. If to be more deeply human is to be intimate, then this special gift of humanness and God alive within us must hallmark our lives. We cannot take the next step to expanding our family identity as a person to a Christian identity without embracing this.

As Christians, we take on an additional name insofar as we belong to a loving, believing and caring community. We are more than just "me," an individual with a family name. Now we can lay claim to another kind of intimacy. Notice that this intimate relationship in terms of what it means to be Christian always speaks in terms of the community as body, and body of Christ. To have a body is to have a story and to take time about it. The story is a familial, communal, and individual journey. To accept Christ is to accept consciously the reality that we are "body people," not only by identity but in our very person, and to work at its implications courageously. Every relationship that comes forth from this carries the potential of being another real witness to God's love for us. This reality is at the very heart of claiming friendship, it is the business of friendship, and it represents a special challenge in today's world of throw-away relationships and disintegrating friendships.

We are basically a divorced society today, because we are embattled and divorced from ourselves. Divorce is not primarily a problem in terms of individuals in marriage. It is at the heart of its reality a problem in the lives of individuals—whether married or single. For too long in the Christian tradition we have taken lightly the reality of laying hold of our own lives and claiming our own intimacy. This must be done before we can discover that for which God has made each of us.

The discovery of what is meant by being intimate and sexual draws on resources deep within us whose existence we have not contended with for a long time. At the very heart of sexuality is the quest for holiness. The deepest attraction within each of us to others must be taken seriously. This call to otherness is a gift, and it always involves risks because it involves the complexity of people in the totality of emotional, personal, and sexual drives.

The issue among most young adults today, particularly singles, is no longer a traditional moral one but rather a search for life's deepest meaning. Is intimacy possible? How is my spiritual journey involved in God's special gift of human sexuality? Is there a deeper meaning to sex and, therefore, to life itself? Before two bodies touch in sexual union, what must happen between two people? Seen by many singles as unacceptable and ultimately destructive of growth is genital expression isolated from a deep human exchange of trust and care. It is true that many others do not raise questions of meaning and context, and simply live from relationship to relationship. However, the central issue for many—married, single, or celibate,—is no longer whether or not to express their sexuality in a genital way. The main question is: What is the role of sexuality in the total process of growth into the fullness of one's self? The implications of this shift for those concerned about intimacy and relationship are profound.

If lived experience is always the rockbed of theology, then the journeys of people, whole or fragile, must be taken as a primary gift for the Christian life and community in any period of time. People journeying and searching, people wrestling with questions of how they can be more deeply human, are really asking how they can be God's people in terms of intimacy and relationships. This searching and questioning must be a journey and process that unfolds throughout life. The process of becoming more deeply human is all of life; every story is important, especially in a time when the wholeness of family and relationships is attacked by confusion about the sacredness of friendship, intimacy and relationships.

In regard to sexuality (intimacy), the traditional moral approach seems to have locked us into a view of sexuality which is predominantly biological. It is true today that we have monitored the psychological developments in terms of sexuality, but the emphasis in Church teaching still remains on biological expression. The birth control debate is an obvious case in point; discussions around minority sexual expressions such as homosexuality are another example. Rarely do the discussions rise above the level of biological concerns. Moreover, traditional sexual morality tends to be individualistic in its orientation, placing the emphasis on moral discernment in terms of oneself. Such discernment stresses the rightness or wrongness of individual acts in terms of a God out there. The larger implications of one's sexuality in terms of the life of the community are rarely addressed. At the very heart of intimacy is otherness. If God created us as body persons in terms of relationships, then the primary focus of this gift needs to be in terms of its communal implications. And it will no longer be adequate that sexuality be situated in terms of the sexual experience in the realm of marriage and family. In this context, the discussion of sexuality becomes an alienating discourse for singles, including the divorced and widowed, as well as for celibates. Sexuality is a gift for everyone; it is at the very heart of life itself and what it means to be made in God's image and likeness.

In America today almost 50% of all Americans live in one-person households. We are becoming a society where the emphasis in terms of family is on the single person living alone. This has challenging implications for what it means to be Christian and for ways in which people claiming this journey as singles need to be more clearly identified in terms of relationships to their families, whether these are spiritual families, blood families or families of friendship. It is the crucial question in terms of the single state, be it transitional or permanent, because one cannot take a celibate lifestyle and retailor it for singles.

Celibacy is a gift and a call no more or less important than the call to marriage or the single state. If this is so, then celibacy is only a gift if it is truly embraced for what it is. It is not a lifestyle chosen either casually or as an unwanted alternative by someone who has not entered into a special relationship. Celibacy, like any state in life, will only be enhanced when it is more clearly focused on and understood as a certain kind of gift to the community at large. There are single persons, living alone or in a family, who have chosen a celibate lifestyle by promise or vow as lay persons. There are others in identical situations who do not think in terms of celibacy but live a chaste lifestyle, and are still searching for significant others in their lives. This does not always lead to marriage and, indeed, large numbers of people more clearly realize today that God calls them to a single lifestyle after they have experienced broken relationships in terms of divorce, separation, or the experience of being discarded in friendship. It will no longer be adequate, in terms of the Christian community, to think in terms of a person's sexual expression being limited to two choices: marriage or celibacy. There are clear nuances for both.

Life experience reveals only too well that becoming more deeply human, more deeply sexual and, therefore, intimate is not something once and for all accomplished. This process is always a quest that continues through all of life. It is never a completed achievement because it is not something happening to me. Rather, at the very heart of that gift is a whole transformation in me in terms of sexuality for the life of the community and the deepening of human relationships. Sexuality can no longer be viewed as a problem to be solved; it is rather a life to be lived, nurtured and celebrated. In this sense, the field of spirituality has become the proper context for viewing sexuality in a full Christian perspective. This, indeed, may be the true sexual revolution of our time.

When individually and together we become increasingly aware of the historical background of our Christian life, we can attain a more comprehensive vantage point regarding the evolution of spirituality and intimacy. This is often best done in terms of oral and written tradition, the tradition of the lives of many men and women who have journeyed the incarnational reality of Christ. Many spiritualities have emerged that are too often cast in terms of one's individual and isolated experience. Many of the stories of the saints measure spiritual growth in terms of the intensity of the inner union with God in prayer, which corresponded to the degree of detachment from the material dimension of human life. To be sure, this view of life witnessed to certain authentic Gospel values, such as single-minded commitment to the Kingdom. Yet, often isolated from the everyday challenges of life, such a spirituality did not form Christians in either the communal or the prophetic dimension of the Christian life. Given this understanding of spirituality, sexuality seen only in its genital expression was logically an impediment to spiritual growth. If one did not lead a celibate life, he/she was at least expected to try to compensate and somehow transcend this "weakness of the flesh." Even the theology of marriage, highly dominated by St. Augustine in Church history, spoke of the conjugal union as something related only to procreation. It was decidedly a lower experience of spiritual possibilities and was merely tolerated. The higher calling was the celibate state. The single state had little or no theological justification, but until recently was seen only as a transition from youth to marriage.

Unless we respond to a communal-centered spirituality that reflects the Church today and the culture in which we live, we will continue to express our experience of sexuality in another era of spirituality. Sexuality needs to be seen in terms of its relational and communal aspects and not in terms of an isolated spiritual search apart from the other dimensions of life. It is no longer adequate to speak in terms of God's special gift of sexuality exclusively in terms of genital behavior. To do so is to contribute to a spiritual wasteland for the community.

Many people today, out of their experience of various sexual attitudes, have begun to articulate a new set of questions and values:

— Sexuality is viewed as our total stance towards life, a way of being and relating to the world as male and female persons.

— Sexuality is seen predominatly as relational, rather than only genital; it is the mode by which we touch others, care, love, and share with them. The distinctions between marriage, single life and celibacy, between homo- and heterosexuality recede into the background. They are not the primary questions in terms of how we are to become more deeply human and intimate. Rather, they are part of the mystery of how God has made each of us—and we still have much to learn in this regard.

— Sexuality is oriented toward the entire process of human integration; it finds its most authentic expression in the realm of the meaning-dimension of life.

— The healthy integration of human sexuality cannot take place outside the orbit of the spiritual dimension of life; there is an integrity to life which must be recognized, embraced and celebrated.

All of creation is seen as profoundly sacred. Human life is filled with crises, namely events which impact our life with a particularly powerful force, moments when life is more transparent before God.

The experience of our sexuality, that is, our ability to relate to others with the fullness of our body-persons, represents one of these crisis moments. It is a moment of growth because the Christian way is intrinsically relational. To be a body-person is to live in relationship with other body-persons. We only know through our bodies. Bodies are God's best gift to us and are meant for loving. I only know myself in relationship to others, and to claim the deepest experience of intimacy is to share that entire life with others. On the other hand, as body-persons, we can relate because we inhabit this particular time and space—herein we share a common quest for meaning. Despite this closeness there is, on the other hand, an absolute "otherness" about each of us. Things around us have meaning only when we refer to them. This dynamic of human relationships supplies us with one of the better paradigms for our relationship with God. God is the absolute other who is, at the same time, more intimate to us than we are to ourselves. We find God precisely in terms of relationship which for us must involve our "body-personness."

The dimensions of intimacy are complex. Just as important is the way that each, over a long period, evokes and nourishes in the other that "contra-sexual" being in each. I speak here of the masculine aspect of a woman, the feminine aspect of the man. We have postponed for too long laying claim and taking hold of the fullest dimension of that otherness even within ourselves. God is not limited to a masculine or feminine personality and the very complexity of God's life within us does not limit it either. For everyone, the orchestration of the complexity of those qualities of femininity and masculinity is essential for this completeness with self, with otherness, and with God. It takes time and courage, even determination and obstinency, to truly embrace and live in our total sexuality and claim its expression to others in intimacy. We will never learn easily or without mistakes, or without being hurt and hurting others. We are returned to the full Christian cycle of things in an understanding of this gift for each of us as single persons—even when that gift is shared in special relationships of friendship or marriage.

The Christian quality of fidelity must be more than an adjective that defines intimacy: It must be the other side of the coin. The one-night-stand for any person is a counter sign to sexual fidelity and hinders the bold prophetic statement we can share with each other in community as intimate persons. The integration of our sexuality, be we single, married or celibate, carries with it profound communal as well as personal implications. Every true encounter with the living God embraces the total gamut of our human existence. The ground is shifting, for the issue of sexuality is no longer whether or not one goes to bed with another person. The prime question becomes: what are the possibilities of intimacy and wholeness for myself, for others, for God's universe? This question has moved the diologue of regarding God's special gift of sexuality to a new sphere, namely to the realm of spirituality where the totality of our lives is the point of what it means to be more deeply human.

Intimacy is at the very heart of everyone's state of life, and when it is not lived to its fullness in terms of communal awareness, then a breakdown of relationships occurs. When this happens, any state in life—marriage, celibacy, singleness—is robbed of the kind of grace and witness that the uniqueness of intimacy with another can bring. Everyone is called to intimacy, living life more deeply human as sexual persons. This will best be done, not by hiding our gift of life and spiritual journey, but by nourishing it always in terms of relationships, aware of God's call to each of us to become whole and, therefore, holy.

FOLLOW UP EXERCISES

1. Think back to the intimate relationships that you have been part of in the last two or three years. Reflect on each in the following areas:
- how this relationship helped me to grow as a person
- how I contributed to the growth of the other person in this relationship
- any aspect of this relationship that I felt was harmful to myself or the other person
- what this relationship helped me to bring to new relationships

2. Look up a definition of intimacy in a dictionary. Is this an adequate description of what intimacy is like for you? If not, add to and expand on the definition.

3. What elements of modern society and culture make developing and sustaining an intimate relationship difficult? Be as specific as possible. Are there any ways in which these factors can be or are being counteracted?

4. What images of intimacy are we presented with? Alone or with friends, make a list of songs, movies, TV shows, etc., that purport to be portraying intimacy between people. Give a summary of the philosophy of each piece of medium, and discuss whether these are images that you wish to adopt for your own relationships with people.

Prayer and Reflection

1. Read 1 John 4:18–19. Reflect on the fears that sometimes make it difficult for you to love others, and the experiences of love that have helped you to overcome these fears.

2. If possible, listen to a recording of "Wherever You Go" by the monks of the Weston Priory (album of the same name). What type of sacrifices does intimacy call us to make for another? How does this apply to your life right now?

Singles
and
Work

One of the interpretations of the Genesis account of the fall is that labor is the result of original sin. Unfortunately, many people today would agree with that evaluation: the nature of their work is such that they feel it must be the result of some evil. Human labor, which at its best should fill us with a feeling of satisfaction and a sense of pride in what we have created, is today too often synonymous with boredom, poor wages, lack of meaning, pressure, indignity, or any of these in varying combinations. Indeed, meaningful work is a critical issue for all persons, especially singles.

How many of us actually see the product that is the result of our work? The oft-cited assembly line worker may be responsible for putting a bolt into place again and again, and has little sense that the finished product is something that he or she helped create. Gone are the days when a person might work with a loom or with tools and create something of which he or she could truly say, "I made this." With the exception of those who make their living at such tasks as carpentry or handicrafts, most of us who do something with our hands and create something from start to finish (knit, sew, make bookcases), do so as a hobby rather than as a means of livelihood.

Rather than bemoan the passing of the "good old days," when life was a lot simpler (and probably a lot more uncomfortable), we would better put our time to use in better understanding some of the contemporary aspects of work, and for our purposes here, how these factors affect single adults.

A major work-related issue of the last century and the beginning of this century was actual working conditions and the remuneration that people received for their jobs. Although in some areas these issues have yet to be resolved justly (the struggle of the farm workers comes to mind), for most of us the conditions in which we work and the money which we receive are not the most important issues we contend with. This is true, of course, for those of us who have jobs. As we saw in Chapter Two, unemployment is a problem for single young adults, particularly for members of minority groups. It can also be a problem for those who appear, on paper, to have every chance of getting a good job. Consider the following examples.

Shelia is a nineteen-year-old Black woman. She dropped out of school during her junior year, when she was sixteen. The law said, she did not have to go to school any more, and there seemed to be no point in continuing high school, which had little relation to anything that was going on in her world. Money was needed at home, so she got a job as a dishwasher in a local restaurant. The pay wasn't great, but it was something. Now, three years later, the restaurant closed and Shelia is out of work. She knows that washing dishes for the rest of her life is not what she wants to do, nor is it going to pay much money. But the job opportunities for high school dropouts are few. She has been out of school for a while now, and is frightened of the idea of going back to school at night to get equivalency diploma. Besides, who wants to be a high school student at the age of nineteen?

Tom just graduated from a good college. He had wanted to be a doctor, but by the time he finished his second year he realized that a B-average was not going to get him into med school. He switched his major and graduated with a degree in sociology. He enjoyed sociology a lot, but there don't seem to be many jobs available to someone with just a bachelor's degree. Teaching is out of the question because he didn't take any education courses and doesn't have a teaching license. He already has a couple of thousand dollars worth of loans to pay off, and doesn't want to borrow more money now to go to graduate school (assuming, of course, that he could get in). He has no typing or other skills, and on the few interviews for clerical jobs that he has gone to, he's been told that he's "overqualified." Translation: they're looking for someone who can type or run office machines, and a college degree is really superfluous.

Sheila and Tom, although they come from very different backgrounds and have very different life experiences, have at least one thing in common: they're out of work. The jobs that either might get are low-paying and would barely (if at all) cover the cost of family and/or financial obligations. Both feel they ought to go back to school, although neither wants to, and besides, will that guarantee anything? And both are very frustrated.

Unemployment, then, is a problem that crosses educational boundaries. Besides the financial problems that unemployment brings, we also need to consider the psychological effects: the time that lays heavily on one's hands, the draining experience of going from interview to interview without results, the often demeaning experience of applying for and receiving public assistance. Add to these the myths that often surround unemployment—that those who don't work really could get jobs but would rather live on public assistance—and we can see that unemployment is a heavy burden to place on anyone, particularly the young, who are told constantly by society that these are indeed "the best years of their lives," and who are bombarded with messages to consume products that are actually luxuries, products that the unemployed can scarcely afford to buy, and are told they can scarcely "afford" to be without.

A similar situation is found among women, newly single through divorce or death of a spouse, who return to work to support themselves and, often, their children. In this decade, the number of households headed by women with no husband present has risen by over two million. If it is difficult to get a job when one has skills and experience, it is more difficult still for a woman who has been out of the job market for a number of years and who, before her marriage, may not have gotten the education or training that may prove helpful in getting a job. Add to this the question of quality child care for a single parent's children, and the issue becomes more complex—and more difficult to find solutions for.

Women, even when they have training and education and have been in the job market for a period of time, are still in the early days of their struggle for equal employment opportunities and equal compensation for work done. Even though some legislation has been passed to insure that women receive the same opportunities and pay as men do, we know from the history of our country that passing a law does not, by any means, insure immediate and total compliance. It will take many years for the ideal envisioned by the law to become a reality. In the meantime, women struggle for the training and educational opportunities, job opportunities, and pay scales which are already possessed by men. Some advances have been made in this area, and as this happens, women are increasingly faced with the same work-related problems that have faced men. What is the nature of the work that I am doing? Does it bring me satisfaction? Does it contribute positively to society? Are the pressures that are part of the job worth the compensation that I receive?

"Money can't buy happiness," we have been told so often, and when we are in financial straits, that saying rings hollow in our ears. But the signs all around us point to the fact that a high-paying job, and the affluence that comes with it, are not necessarily the end of our problems; they may well be just the beginning.

All of us are probably acquainted with someone (most likely a man, since at this point, men are more likely to be holding high-paying, high-pressure jobs) who's had an ulcer, or a coronary, or some other stress-related illness at a very early age. (It is not uncommon for this to be happening to people when they are still in their thirties.) While many factors combine to produce such a situation, it is not uncommon for this to occur in a person who has a financially rewarding, but stress-producing job. The work may not even be something that the person enjoys doing. Nevertheless, work is work, it has to be done, and at some point we may become so involved in the *doing* that the actual content of what we are trying to accomplish gets lost in the shuffle. Further, the financial rewards of success propel us on an upward spiral of the goods and the kind of lifestyle that such wealth can obtain for us. A new car, a bigger and better vacation, property, a few more shares of stock—these things are in themselves neither good nor bad. What determines their value is what we do with them and the price we pay (monetarily and otherwise) to gain them. Money, it is true, cannot buy happiness—but in today's world it can buy us things that will, at least for a while, bring us pleasure.

The single person may find him or herself tempted to invest more and more time and energy into work, if for no other reason than that there are fewer family commitments to which the single person is responsible. Many single people see work as their primary commitment at this point in their lives. It is precisely to these people—the young, "unattached," upwardly mobile of today's society, that many advertisers appeal with their pitches for products and goods that are signs of "the good life. It is important, therefore, that singles have a context in which to examine the work that they do, its advantages, and its disadvantages.

Of particular concern to us here is the number of single lay people who work as professionals within the Church itself. For such people, affluence is hardly a problem; most people who work for the Church must instead cope with the problems of a wage that is not commensurate with their education, training and labor. We are living in a time when, for the first time in history, the work force within the Church is shifting from one that is predominantly religious and clerical to one that is increasingly lay. This shift brings with it a change in the economic picture. This is not offered as an excuse for the injustices that lay employees may have suffered, but it does give some insight into some of the reasons that have contributed to this.

I spoke recently to a priest who is the pastor of a rather poor parish in an urban diocese. As badly as his parish is doing financially, the school is solvent and is run almost entirely on the money it receives from tuition. I thought that perhaps the tuition fees were rather exhorbitant, but when he quoted a figure, it was the same as most other schools in the diocese. What enabled the school to survive was the fact that over half the faculty were sisters. This situation is unusual, and it is not mentioned as a plea for the return of things to the way they used to be. What this situation does point out is that "the way things used to be" exists in very few places, and that number is dwindling rapidly. What we need to face is the fact that things have changed—no matter what the reasons we give, or whether we see the causes as good or bad. And until we face these changes and learn to live with them, we are doing a great injustice to lay people who work for the Church.

The fact that there are increasing numbers of lay people on a Church staff—whether it be on a faculty or parish team—means that there are going to be economic changes that *in justice* have to be addressed and dealt with. These include such issues as a just wage—a wage that is commensurate with a person's education, experience, and the job that he or she is currently doing—on which a person can reasonably live. No one enters Church work because it is the best place to make one's first million, but this is no reason to expect people to live on salaries that are not in keeping with today's cost of living. It also means that we have to be attentive to issues that were previously attended to by a parish or religious community: just benefits in terms of such things as medical coverage and retirement plans. It also means an adequate system for redress of grievances and a clearly stated policy regarding job security. The days when sister or father went where a superior said to go, and stayed there until a superior said it was time to leave have long since ended for religious and priests, and we should not expect such a system to be practiced by lay people.

Assuming that such basic issues are resolved justly (and in many cases that seems, unfortunately, to lay in the future) there are other important issues for lay people who work within the Church that need to be addressed. Many lay people within the Church today find themselves enmeshed in a clerical caste system in which, by definition, they are at the bottom of the ladder. The final word in any theological, pastoral, or educational discussion may belong to father —although the lay person's education and experience may make him or her far more competent to answer the question. If this is true for lay people in general, it is especially true for lay ministers.

The reason that these issues of Church-related work are so important to us here is that many of the lay people who work within the Church are single. As we have noted above, the wage situation may be such that only a single person, with no one else to support, may be able to afford to work for what the Church pays. Many dedicated lay people have reluctantly moved into another area of work when marriage and family responsibilities made living on a ministerial salary impossible. Others are able to continue their work only with some degree of personal sacrifice.

Another problem that we face is the ironic situation that officials of the Church, while on the one hand wondering where all the young, single people have gone, are sometimes guilty of taking for granted the young, single people who are in their employ. Often decisions are made and energy is expended in trying to "reach" singles who no longer participate in Church life, without consulting with single people within the Church.

Lay people who work within the Church, particularly singles, are faced with a myriad of issues that often militate against the work that they have chosen to do. Their wages and benefits are often not in keeping with all that the Church itself has said about a just wage. The system within the Church is such that, in addition to not receiving monetary recognition, the lay person does not experience equality with his or her clerical colleagues. The single person who works for the Church often realizes that he or she is working for an institution that is, for the most part, ignoring the needs of his or her peer group.

The issues raised here about work—whether it is work for the Church or work in what used to be called "the world"—are complex and will not be solved in a superficial discussion. We can, however, identify a set of critical questions that will help the Church identify better the issues that it needs to address.

What do we as a Church really say about work and money?

We may be just as guilty as everyone else in fostering a sense of competitiveness in people and in valuing people in terms of what they do. I recently came across an announcement in a parish bulletin that had to do with an associate pastor who was being made pastor of a neighboring parish. The paragraph in the bulletin was written by the pastor of that community, and in it he was congratulating the new pastor on his "promotion" and describing being a pastor as "every priest's dream." Change the terminology a little, and it could just as easily have been the announcement of a promotion in any major corporation. What must people think when they read things like that?

As a Church whose founder said that his kingdom was "not of this world," what do we actually communicate about money? Are appeals for money, as important as these may be, overshadowing the preaching of the Gospel at our liturgies? How much of the respect that we accord people is determined by their financial status or the contributions which they make to the Church? What does the lifestyle of those who represent the Church say about money and material goods?

What do we as a Church say to and about those who do not work?

By our silence, we can support the myths and misunderstandings that surround unemployment and public assistance, or we can help our people to understand the effects of unemployment on an individual or a family. Are there projects in our community that exist to help the unemployed, or to create jobs? If so, how can we support these? Perhaps most importantly, we can help people to see that while the Church is concerned with *charity*—giving of its resources to those who are in need—it is equally concerned with *justice*—working to change structures that are hurting people.

How do we as a Church treat the people whom we employ?

The issues here are almost endless, and we have examined some of the most basic problems earlier. Each particular community needs to examine its attitude toward those lay people who work for it. A secondary question from this examination is how we treat volunteers who work in our midst. We can learn a lot about our attitudes toward work by looking at how we regard those whose labor is not rewarded with a salary.

Much of what we have said here is applicable to all people, not just singles. We have tried to highlight some of the issues that are of particular importance to single people. When all is said and done, the basic issue is one of credibility. Many single people today are disenchanted with the attitudes conveyed by society with regard to work and money. They have heard all the old cliches about the dog-eat-dog business world, looking out for number one, working one's way to the top (often by stepping on someone else), etc. What they are listening for is a "second opinion" on all of this. Is there a better attitude to have toward one's work and one's money? Is there really a price for everything and everyone? If the Church could speak and act credibly in this area, it might pave the way for singles to hear a more profound answer to the questions of labor and money—and it might also be the issue that convinces singles that the Church does care about their experiences and their needs.

FOLLOW UP EXERCISES

1. Evaluate your present work situation on a scale of 1 to 5, with 1 denoting a great deal of dissatisfaction and 5 a great deal of satisfaction.
My labor is meaningful
I am paid a just wage
I am able to use my natural skills and talents
I can grow in my ability to relate with others
I am making a contribution to my society
My work effort is acknowledged by my superiors
My work has enabled me to learn new skills
My total work load is such that I have free time to pursue other goals and activities.

Are there any areas in which I scored a 1 or 2? If so, is there anything I can do to improve the situation? What is one concrete step I can take?

If possible, have a friend or friends evaluate their work situations and discuss common problems and possible solutions.

2. How do I judge the value of a job? (Check as many as apply.)
    by the number of people who can do the same job
    by the financial remuneration
    by the value given by society to the job
    by the amount of training or education needed to do it
    by the end result of the job
    by the essential nature of the job
    by how the person doing the job feels about it

How do your answers affect your feelings about your own job? About your self-worth? If you experience a sense of valuelessness about your work, is that due to the job itself or the attitudes attached to it?

Prayer and Reflection

1. Try to become familiar with Church teaching on the nature of work. How does this contrast with the world's attitude toward work?

The basic document in this area is *Rerum Novarum*, the 1891 encyclical of Leo XIII on the Rights and Duties of Capital and Labor. It can be found in *Seven Great Encyclicals,* published by Paulist Press. Related encyclicals include *Quadragesimo Anno* by Pius XI; *Mater et Magister* by John XXIII; and *Populorum Progressio* by Paul VI.

2. Read Matthew 6:26–34. Do you consider this "practical" advice? How can the attitude described here be incorporated into daily living?

The
Church
and
Singles

Up to now, we have looked mainly at areas that are of importance to singles, and talked a little about how the Church can speak credibly and compassionately in these areas. Now it is time to examine the Church's relationship to singles and the attitude which the Church has toward the single population. If the Church affirms the importance of the single population through words and deeds, only then will it speak credibly on the issues we have discussed. In Chapter Two we looked briefly at four major areas in this regard; now it is time to examine them in more depth.

Evangelization.

Like any idea whose time has come, evangelization runs the risk of becoming the latest fad, or a catchall that is supposed to solve all problems and tie up all loose ends. It is important that we be clear on what evangelization is, and what it can and cannot do.

In 1978, the USCC Department of Education's Office of Campus and Young Adult Ministry sponsored six regional conferences across the country and a national symposium at Merrimack College in Massachusetts, all on the topic of evangelization. One of purposes of these regional conferences, and the national conference on evangelization of young adults that followed, was to examine what the encyclical on evangelization was actually saying, and then applying it to ministry with young adults. *Evangelii Nuntiandi (On Evangelization in the Modern World)* was issued on December 8, 1975, and history will probably judge it to be one of the most important documents of Pope Paul VI's papacy. However, the document will have little value to us if we talk about it and what we think it says, rather than speaking from a careful reading and real study of the encyclical.

Running through the encyclical is the view that evangelization is a basic element of Christian life, an activity that all Christians participate in. The encyclical warns against limiting evangelization "to one sector of mankind or to one class of people or to a single type of civilization" (par. 50); it describes evangelization as ". . . a complex process made up of varied elements: the renewal of humanity, witness, explicit proclamation, inner adherence, entry into the community, acceptance of signs, apostolic initiative . . . ," process that are "mutually enriching" (par. 24). The witness of life is of primary importance; such witness should ". . . stir up irresistible questions in the hearts of those who see how they (Christians) live: Why are they like this? Why do they live in this way? What or who is it that inspires them? Why are they in our midst?" (par. 21).

The entire document is rich with images and principles that cover the areas of the content of evangelization, its methods, beneficiaries, workers, and spirit. The document has many applications, but we can see from just the few ideas and passages mentioned here that there is much food for thought for those who are involved in any way with single adults. As we have seen, this group has often been ignored or slighted by the Church; the Pope's warning about limiting the scope of evangelization is well taken here. Likewise, the stress on witness as a primary means of evangelizing is of concern to us here. It is such living witness on the part of the Church that is going to invite single adults to a closer look at what the Church is all about. Preaching at people is not going to do this. (It will probably have the reverse effect.) Social programs, however low key and well intentioned, are not going to do this. (Such activities are better carried on by people in the secular world who have expertise in this area.) In the course of my work with single and young adults, I have had the opportunity to talk with many people who are working in these areas, whether in an official capacity (diocesan director, parish coordinator) or in some other way. The people I have talked to and visited with have been a diverse group, and, as might be expected, so have been their approaches to their work. The common denominator among all of them, however, has been the general premise that has guided the beginnings of their work. Those who are leading successful ministries to single and young adults have begun by getting to know people on a somewhat informal basis. (This seems awfully obvious, until you consider the number of people who try to initiate a ministry by holding a meeting with people they don't know, or who expect a first gathering of singles to attract one hundred people, all of whom are raring to go.) In the course of such getting-to-know others, basic concerns emerge—relationships with peers, loneliness, sexuality, work, one's relationship with God and/or the Church. Such information is exchanged over coffee, over pot luck suppers, at home, in places where single adults gather. It is only when friendships begin to form and trust is established that we can begin to talk about more structured programs and activities—and these must always be in response to real needs. The person who is in ministry with single and young adults invites others, by his or her person and way of life, to become acquainted and to talk about issues that are of importance. The successful single and young adult ministers I have met are living examples of what *Evangelii Nuntiandi* is all about; their lived experience bears out what Pope Paul VI summarized for us in his letter. When single and young adults gathered at the six regional conferences and the national meeting in 1978, it was precisely to share this lived experience and to discuss its meaning and the ways in which the experience can be deepened and enriched.

Evangelization is a word we have heard a lot about recently, and which we will continue to hear spoken and discussed. We need to understand what the word means, and this can best be accomplished by an understanding of the encyclical. We must also be careful to differentiate evangelization from catechesis (see below), and to incorporate the principles set forth in *Evangelii Nuntiandi* into our work with single adults.

Adult catechesis.
We have noted that there is a difference between evangelization and catechesis—an important difference that is sometimes overlooked. Evangelization might generally be defined as "proclaiming the Gospel to the people of today," a phrase that Pope Paul VI uses in the first paragraph of his encyclical, although he warns against ". . . any partial and fragmentary definition which attempts to render the reality of evangelization in all its richness, complexity and dynamism" (par. 17). Generally, we think of evangelization as preceding catechesis, as a first proclamation of good news to people who have not heard it. The obvious implication of this is that evangelization is an activity that takes place in what used to be known as "mission territory." An unfortunate corollary of this is that evangelization is confined to the missions. One of the great contributions of the Pope's encyclical on evangelization is that he reminds us that evangelization is not an activity that is the sole prerogative of missionaries who work in foreign lands, as important as this work is. Evangelization, as we have seen, is an activity that is the right and duty of all Christians, and whose beneficiaries are far greater in scope than we may have previously imagined.

Having said all of this, what is the place of catechesis in the Church, and in particular, how does it relate to single adults? Again, catechesis is a word that we have allowed ourselves to define too narrowly. We have equated catechesis with education, and that is good, *if* we think of education in its broadest sense. Our allocation of resources and personnel testifies to the fact that we have limited our idea of education to formal institutions of learning that reach children and adolescents, and that percentage of the population that goes on to study at a Catholic college.

Besides the fact that most of our educational resources are being invested in the below 18 population, there is another by-product of this concentration on the young that we should examine. If a parish has a strong investment in childhood education through the staffing and maintainance of a parish school, the investment does not stop there. The cost of operating such a school—maintaining the building, heating it, paying a faculty that is composed increasingly of lay people who must be paid a living wage—spirals every year. Fund raising activities will often center around the school. Parents' associations are an important part of the school's life. In short, not only is the school per se a prominent part of parish life, but the parish may find many of its adult activities directed at the parents of school children. The obvious result of this is that the time, money, and other resources needed for activities for single adults will suffer.

It is not being suggested here that Catholic grammar and high schools should close up shop. They perform a valuable service and are here to stay in one form or another. What we need to examine is the initial presupposition that the main beneficiaries of our educational efforts ought to be the young. This is important to delve into for several reasons, of importance to single adults and married adults alike.

If we are concerned about passing on the faith to our children, then we ought to realize that the Catholic school is not reaching all of them. The Catholic school is only one place where catechesis happens. Those children who do not attend such schools, for whatever reason, have the same need for catechesis—and this need must be addressed.

Secondly, we do no favor to the parents of our children if we provide the best in catechetical instruction for their offspring and do not offer similar opportunities for adults. Anyone who has, for example, prepared children for the sacraments can tell you how difficult it can be to meet with parents whose own religious education effectively ended ten or fifteen years ago when they finished Catholic school. The truths of our faith have not changed, but our understanding of them and our expression of them has evolved, particularly in the years since the Second Vatican Council. It is a sad commentary on our times that children often understand these changes better than adults do, because children are the ones to whom we have offered the best of our catechetical skills.

The parent whose child goes to Catholic school or religious instruction often encounters a graced moment to grow in faith, a moment that begins when the parent goes to a meeting, reads a book, or talks to a catechist in an effort to understand better what little Johnny or Mary is being taught. The single adult, unless he or she is a parent, does not have this opportunity. In many parishes, unfortunately, it may be the only opportunity for an adult to delve more deeply into his or her own faith.

So much of what Jesus says and does in the Gospel makes sense in a far deeper way when we reach adulthood than it did when we first heard of it as children. So many of the events of adult life—a major career or life change, the death of a parent or loved one, a serious illness of our own, reaching a thirtieth or fortieth birthday, achieving financial success and wondering about its value—are the raw material out of which we examine our own lives, the dreams that have been realized, the promises we have not kept, the sense of our own mortality. It is out of these experiences that we can come to the Gospel, not in search of facts to be learned, but in quest to understand better our own journey in life. Adulthood, then, is a new catechetical moment when we need not so much a set of facts as a way of understanding, not an instructor but others with whom to discuss and share our thoughts and experiences.

The "world" has understood that adults need opportunities for new ways of understanding, and so almost everywhere we go we read about adult education, centers for "lifelong learning," and other attempts to meet this need. Some of the course offerings may be just for fun, some may sound rather silly, but the philosophy behind such attempts is important: that education does not end with schooling; that adults want and need the opportunity to come together to enrich their lives.

If this is true on the level of matters such as home repair and the new math, how much more so is it when we are talking about something as important as religious values. The single person is especially in need of such opportunities. He or she may live alone, without the context of developing a conversation with someone after dinner, or in place of a television show. The nature and pace of business is such that it is often not the place for anything more than the most practical of conversations.

Certainly a strong case can be made for the Church to broaden its horizons with regard to catechesis. Some local communities are doing just that. A variety of frameworks must be considered—everything from instructional type courses to help people update their knowledge of Scripture and Church teachings to smaller, more informal gatherings that revolve around praying together, reading Scripture or discussing topics of interest. Our problem is not a lack of ideas of what might be done; rather, our problem has been a lack of insight and imagination regarding what catechesis is and what the needs of adult Christians are.

Lay single leadership.

It has been noted that one of the problems of local communities vis-a-vis singles is that many opportunities for involvement are directed, however unconsciously, at married adults, particularly those with children. By no means is it being suggested that the Church ought to get involved in the business of quotas. However, in developing opportunities for lay leadership within the Church (which for most people will mean the parish), we must always be aware of including a variety of people, among them single adults.

The single adult who comes to Church, hears a sermon that assumes that "family" means husband, wife, and children, sees the lay ministries of lector and extraordinary minister of the Eucharist being exercised by married people, and hears of Church-sponsored activities that are again directed at the married and those with children, will receive a message about the Church's attitude toward singles that makes a far deeper impression than any words we might speak. Even something so seemingly harmless as selling tickets to parish social activities at x dollars per couple bespeaks a very clear attitude about how we view the world. To sponsor, in the climate described above, a somewhat token meeting for "single adults, age twenty-one and over," is going to make little headway in showing single adults that we care—and with little wonder.

Any attempt to address the specific needs of single adults must be balanced by a conscious attempt to invite them and include them in the total life of the parish. Otherwise, these efforts to "do something for single people" will be perceived as just that—something done to fulfill our obligation, while in the meantime all the rest of parish life procedes unchanged. Likewise, these events for singles that seem to have as their sole purpose the gathering of Catholic singles in one place seems to suggest that we see singles as merely needing to meet other Catholic singles so that they can pair up and marry. While in fact some such relationships may result from such programs, this should never be their reason for existence.

One reason that we have not responded adequately to the single adults in our midst is that we (and here I mean the clergy, predominantly) have assumed that *we* know what singles want and need, rather than listening to our single population. Many diocese sponsor days of recollection for their priests. These days are planned by the priests themselves, who form a committee to work out the details. No priest would accept the idea that such a day be planned in its entirety by the lay people of the diocese (although that might prove very interesting!)

By the same token, priests should not be surprised when single people do not look favorably on having their needs determined by the clergy.

A common response to this idea is the cry that it is hard to identify who the single adults are. If leadership among single adults were nurtured, this would not be a problem. Any outreach must start somewhere, and the main place to begin is simply talking to the single people in the neighborhood whom you can identify, whether they are active in the parish or not. Such conversation does not begin with a discussion of whether the person is involved in any way in the Church. Making the needs of the Church known—rather than assuming that singles have a set of needs and are waiting for the Church to address them—may be the best place to start.

Many people—single and married alike—will become involved when they are invited to do so. It is interesting to speculate on how many of the apostles would have taken the initiative to follow Jesus if he had not invited them first. No doubt there were some he invited who said, "Thanks, but no thanks," and we should not be surprised if some of our invitations meet with the same response. Not knowing what response we will get is the risk we take when we speak to people as persons, rather than relying on an impersonal appeal in the parish bulletin.

Once singles become involved in the life of the Church, it is essential that such involvement not become a source of unmitigated frustration. This is true of all lay leadership in general. Too often lay people take the risk of becoming involved in leadership only to find that their role amounts to not much more than that of glorified "go-fers." There is much room in the Church for lay people to become actively involved in making decisions that affect the life of their community.

When single people (in the plural—not just one or two token members) become actively involved in the life of the community, the needs and gifts of single people will become more and more apparent. The question, "What do singles need?" as asked by the parish clergy or staff will be replaced with an atmosphere in which a ministry with single adults will be as natural a part of Church life as are ministry with married people and parents at the present time. Such a situation, unfortunately, is still in the future, and much work needs to be done in this regard. We worry, and with good reason, about the declining number of single people who are found in the pews on Sunday and on parish rosters. Were we to begin to make an effort to make the Church a place where single people can feel at home, we would be taking a big step in addressing those who feel alienated from the Church in a very profound sense.

Singles speak to the Church.

Single people are speaking to the Church in a variety of ways. Those single people who are no longer affiliated with the Church in a formal way are speaking to us by their absence. As we have seen earlier, disaffiliation with the institution is never to be presumed as a sign of disinterest in God or spiritual matters. The reasons for disaffiliation are legion, and may range from the newly singled person who feels the Church does not welcome the divorced to the person who has genuine problems with a particular teaching of the Church. We will never know what those reasons are unless we listen. Obviously, we are not going to hear them on the steps of the Church after Sunday mass. This means broadening our understanding of who and where the Church is.

It is important to keep in mind that not every single person whom we speak with or whose life we touch is going to make an immediate re-entry into the life of the official Church. If our purpose in ministering with singles is to get them back on the roll books, then we have missed the point of what ministry is all about. At different points in their lives, people have different spiritual needs and their own understanding of how these needs are best met. A particular person may not see the institution as meeting those needs at this point in life. That decision is not ours to judge, and certainly it does not mean that we should not continue to listen to people and welcome them when they do participate in the life of the Church.

Singles have been a minority group in society and in the Church for a long time. Like any minority group that is growing in numbers and in prominence, they are making their needs and gifts known. It is very tempting for those within the institution to assume knowledge of what those needs and gifts are, or to attempt to dictate the ways in which dialogue can take place. Any conversation between the Church (in the person of its representatives, whether clergy or lay) and single people should not be an opportunity for the Church to defend its track record with singles (a difficult task in some respects!) or to convince singles of the rightness or wrongness of particular positions. Such a dialogue is a moment for real listening, a time for putting aside our own personal agenda to hear what the other is saying to us.

Single people live in a world that is, all of a sudden, sitting up and taking notice. Consequently, singles are being told how to recreate, how to get ahead, how to behave sexually, how to cure their loneliness, how to cure their boredom, how to lead the "good life." The responses that the culture gives singles make it obvious that very little listening is being done to what singles are *really* saying. Our culture has told singles, time and again, that material goods, sex appeal, and youth are the "answers." In truth, the questions—about the fundamental meaning of life, the need for intimacy, meaningful work, friendships of substance, and self-respect—have gone unanswered, or have been answered with very temporary solutions.

It is a great temptation for the Church to jump on the cultural bandwagon and try to duplicate, in a "catholic" way, what society is doing. Or it can listen to the real questions, respond to them out of the context of the Gospel, and be a source of genuine support and community. As the Church becomes more aware of its ministry with single adults in this decade, we are taking the first steps in deciding what that ministry will be.

FOLLOW UP EXERCISES

1. Make a list of the issues that you feel the Church ought to be addressing with regard to single adults. Next to each item, write down what your local church is doing specifically in this regard. If no response is being made, list one step that you feel can be made in this area.

2. Using your list as a basis of discussion, brainstorm with friends to find out their reactions to this issue and what the church is doing/not doing. Decide if there is some action you can take as a group to make the local church aware of your gifts and needs.

3. Investigate the possibility of having an all-day or weekend session on "Single Adults and the Church." Discuss topics to be addressed, resources persons, and opportunities for prayer and liturgy.

Prayer and Reflection
1. "I have called you by name—you are mine" (Is. 43:1). What does it mean to me now to be called in so intimate a way by God? What does it mean to be part of the people whom he has called his own?

2. Read and become familiar with *Evangelii Nuntiandi* (On Evangelization in the Modern World) by Pope Paul VI. In what ways is evangelization a need in my life? In what way do I evangelize others?

3. Set aside a period of time each day for spiritual reading and/or updating your understanding of the faith. Consider keeping a journal in which you record your own spiritual journey.

79

Singles:
A
Look
at
the
Future

Any look at the state of singles in society today, and in particular, in the Church, would not be complete without some suggestions, however brief and general, about what the single experience will mean for the future. What we don't need are predictions; what we do need are some observations that will serve as guides for us as the Church moves into the twenty-first century.

There are two points of view that are willing to write off any meaningful relationship between the Church and the single population. The first is found among those singles who feel that the Church will never say or be anything that is relevant to singles. This is based on past experience, and does not allow any room for growth and development in the Church's approach. The second point of view exists within the Church itself, and is found among those who feel that singles are not an important part of the people of God. Such an attitude is the result of a misunderstanding about what being single means, and a real refusal to listen to what single people are saying about themselves and their lives.

Assuming that these two viewpoints are erroneous, what kind of relationship between singles and the Church at large is possible and desirable? What vision are we working with in our ministry with single adults?

In the first place, the data seem to indicate that, at least for a while, we are going to be dealing with a society that will have a significant number of single adults, whether divorced, separated, widowed, or never married. In terms of age, a growing number of these people will fall into the category of early adulthood. This is significant for institutions, especially for the Church at the local level (the parish), which at the present time is family oriented. This is not to say that the parish should abandon its ministry to and its concern for families. The disinterest that singles have suffered is not going to be justly remedied by concentrating on singles to the exclusion of everyone else. What is important is that the parish broaden its concept of who its population is. A fair number of people will continue to be married couples, some of whom will have children. However, even as the parish ministers to this group, it has to broaden its ministerial base to include singles. A few of the issues that concern singles and some of the needs of single people will be quite similar to those of married couples. However, as we have seen, some of the needs and critical issues of singles are unique to this particular group. It is these issues and needs that must be addressed by the local community, a community that has first listened to the single people in its midst.

A recent issue of *Psychology Today* reported the results of a reader survey that it did on friendship (October 1979). Not surprisingly, one of the key factors that militate against the development of friendship is loneliness. One of the main commodities offered to singles, as we have noted, is a context in which social activities and interaction with others can take place, whether this be through vacation plans, bars, dances, or the like. What we have also seen is that such social situations do not guarantee (and in some ways actually work against) the development of real friendships and a sense of genuine community. That a society that offers so many ways to "get together" can still produce so many people hungry for real friendship should make us stop and take a long look at what is actually going on. This situation is the antithesis of everything that the Christian community stands for. Our task for the future then is not to produce more social activities for the sake of social activities. That is being done by someone else, and it is not solving the real problem. The question is how the Christian community responds to the need for friendship and community.

In the past, the extended family took care of many of the friendship and community needs of the people in its midst. As the nuclear family replaces the extended family (for good or ill), this source of a sense of community and belonging disappears. What the commune movement of the sixties taught us is that the role that the extended family once played can be assumed in some way by a family that is not based on blood kinship. That so many of our young people joined such communes says something about the then-heralded ideal family, consisting of mother, father, 2.4 children and two cars.

Communes that were in any way successful and were able to last for any period of time did so because the members had common goals, common values, and a sense of commitment to the group. We see this in a dangerous extreme in religious cults and similar monolithic groups. As unattractive as such groups may be to us, we see in them some inkling of the importance of human solidarity in an impersonal world. We are also challenged to consider broader definition of families.

A factor of further significance to us is that a large number of members of groups such as Hare Krishna are young people who were raised as Roman Catholics. (Some estimate that as many as fifty percent of those belonging to Krishna groups are Catholic.) It is possible to draw many tentative conclusions from this, but the least we can say is that such groups are meeting some needs that organized religion has not adequately addressed. One clue might lie in the fact that people who have belonged to such groups were in part first attracted by the personal attention that was shown to them by "recruiters." What can all of these observations tell us about what the Church needs to be doing in the future?

In the first place, we need to be gathering *small* groups of people in which individuals can be affirmed in their own identity and in their membership in the group. The days in which we measured the "success" of our Scripture study group or prayer meeting by the number of people who filled the parish auditorium are long since over. Even the large groups that have sprung up in our midst (Charismatic communities come to mind) recognize that large groups must be broken down into smaller groups.

What is so important about small groups, and in particular why are they important in ministry with single adults? Several factors come to mind. It seems that much that happens in our society takes place in one of two extreme ways—faceless crowds or lonely anonymity. One clear example is going to and from one's place of employment. When we think of an urban area, for example, one of two means of transportation comes to mind. People are either crammed into trains, subways, or buses, surrounded by strangers, being touched and jostled by people they don't even know. Or the harried commuter is driving alone in his or her car, caught in a traffic jam, surrounded by hundreds of other people, each of whom sits alone in an automobile. While not everything in life happens this way, it seems that we are more often than not caught in one of these two extremes in our day to day living. The single person feels this even more acutely if he or she comes home to a house or apartment shared with no one, perhaps to read a magazine or watch a television show that is designed for a person who desn't exist—the "average single."

Whether we are alone or in a particular setting, or jammed together with a large group of people, no genuine sharing or communication can take place. This situation unfortunately often carries over into the life of the believing community, where the sheer size of a local community can work against people's coming to know each other and develop a real sense of community. In seeking to gather small groups of "base communities," we seek to eliminate some of the barriers that are imposed, in their own ways, by both solitude and crowds.

The importance of small groups is that they provide, first and foremost, a setting in which people can get to know other people—their names, their occupations, something about their lifestyles—in short, the kind of information that people need to exchange before we can talk about sharing on a deeper level. People can also get to know more people in a small group setting than they can in a larger context. In a large group it is tempting to talk to one or two people and for this sub-group to then become the "port in the storm" of all those other strange faces. (Anyone, for example, whose first class in college was a lecture with 250 other students can attest to the strength of this dynamic.) In a small group, that pressure is removed, and people can interact with each other more easily.

A second reason for forming small groups is that people's needs—even the needs of those who can be grouped together under a broad, general heading like "single adult"—are very different. We have looked at the different ways of being single and seen that there is no such thing as the "classic" or "average" single. If this is the case, then people need to further group themselves according to particular needs. Younger single adults, for example, who are still in school or who are just beginning their careers will have a very different set of concerns from older single adults who are established in their work, perhaps own their own homes, perhaps have children. This is not to say that these two groups have nothing to say to one another. But we do need to recognize the fact that we cannot treat these two groups as if their concerns and their needs are identical. To attempt to "do something" for singles without recognizing such diversity is inviting failure. Such an attempt will fail, not because of lack of genuine interest on the part of singles, but because presuming to speak to everyone usually means that we are speaking to no one.

The outreach to single adults that is catching fire among singles is outreach that does not attempt to be a "program" that is going to have something for everyone. It is ministry that begins with one-to-one contact with singles and centers around low-key kinds of activities—pot luck suppers, wine and cheese parties and the like. It is through such activities that people get to know each other and trust each other and begin to build a sense of community. Only when such trust and community begin to develop can people begin to talk about deeper issues like God, Church, intimacy, and sexuality. And when this happens, it is not a case of some "expert" talking *at* single adults, but rather single adults sharing their experience and their journeys with each other.

Many of the people involved in initiating such ministry are themselves single lay people. It may take real humility for the institutional Church to admit that the most effective responses to the needs and concerns of singles may not come from having the local priest sponsor a program. Ministry with singles is a particular area in which the Church has a real opportunity to develop and encourage lay ministry and peer group ministry. That this is beginning to happen on the grass roots level is an encouraging sign and one that should be encouraged and supported by the institution wherever and whenever possible.

Developing ministry with single adults will bring with it benefits not only to singles themselves but to the Church at large. Before we discuss these it is important to remember that the Church should view its ministry with singles as an act of justice. We have seen that we have too long ignored both the unique needs of singles and the gifts that they can bring to the Church. To remedy this situation is to do nothing less than follow the gospel mandate that the good news be preached to all people.

As we enter the 1980s, whose first year has been designated by the bishops of the United States as the "Year of the Family," it is especially important that the Church keep its single members in the forefront of its consciousness. The growing number of one-parent and single-person families has forced us to rethink and redefine our notion of family. In doing so we need to remember that all single people—whether living alone without children, or living with parents but perhaps too old to be thought of as "children"—are part of the Church's concern when it speaks about families and their development. To take concrete steps to minister to and with singles must be part of this concern.

We should not delude ourselves by thinking that ministry with singles is only a case of the Church "doing for" single people. Single people have, first of all, a witness to offer to the Church. Singles are living out the call to be Christian in a way that is different from marriage or priesthood and religious life, but in a way that has its own distinct value. When the Church listens to that witness and takes it to heart, it is receiving a most precious gift.

There is so much in our world that stresses and glorifies being part of a twosome that the message we receive oftentimes that it is better to be part of a couple—no matter what the particulars—than to be "alone." The result of this is that *any* relationship, no matter how exploitive or destructive to the parties concerned, can appear preferable to being without a partner. If the church esteems the singles in its midst, then we not only respect the single vocation, we also affirm the sacredness of human relationships. We give witness to the fact that relationships with other human beings, especially the intimate relationship we call marriage, are not something we enter into lightly. If being single has a good and positive value, then it is not something we avoid at any cost—even when the price is a destructive relationship.

Our concept of personhood will deepen when we affirm the value of being single. It is very easy, in our society, to define someone's worth in terms of some extrinsic factor—a job, possessions, wealth, spouse. To afirm the value of the single state is to affirm something that we already believe—that a person's worth and value is dependent on nothing extrinsic to the person. Our value as persons comes simply from the fact that we are human beings created by God in his image. Ultimately, everything else is relative to that.

Finally, when the Church really welcomes single adults into its midst, it will find that it has welcomed people with energy, talent, and unique spiritual journeys that the Church needs to hear about. If we think of ministry with singles as another program, another expense, another group that "wants something" from us, then that attitude will be apparent and we will not really be welcoming anyone. Only when we begin to think of single people as a real part of the Church will ministry with singles make any sense.

Ever since the Christian community began there have been questions about who is really a part of it. Peter and Paul disagreed over the role on Gentiles in the early community, and since then our history has been dotted with discussion, sometimes heated, over the place and role of various groups within the community. In a sense, we should not expect our age to be any different. However, in all of this the model we must keep in mind is that of Jesus, who did not parcel out places at his table according to any type of sociological survey. He welcomed always those who were poor, which quite simply meant those who were without power, understanding, and hearing. Certainly in our day, single adults fall into that category because we have not listened to them and cared for them.

The Sunday congregation is made up almost entirely of children, older adults, and married couples. "Where are the single people?" somebody asks. Perhaps it is time to answer that question by welcoming single adults to the place that is already rightfully theirs.

FOLLOW UP EXERCISES

1. List the communities to which you belong. Which of these would you consider a "base community"? Write down the qualities that make it so.

2. What needs in your life can be met by a small group of people who care about you? What needs of others can you meet? Write these down and compare with the qualities you listed above. Can you draw any conclusions from this?

3. Commitment to Christ and his community involves outreach to others. Some social thinkers have described the past decade as fostering excessive concern with oneself. Which statement more accurately describes your orientation at this point? Is there any way in which you feel you can become more involved in service to others?

Prayer and Reflection

1. This chapter points out the importance of friendship and the factors that militate against it. Read John 15:11-17 and reflect on the following:
   - the characteristics of friendship that Jesus presents
   - which of these qualities is most important to you at this point in your life
   - the barriers you encounter in developing and exercising that particular quality

2. For prayer and reflection in a small group, ask each person to bring a song, poem or short reading that best describes what friendship means to him/her. Share these and discuss. You might close with a reading of John 15:11–17, using the reflection points noted above.